The Single Guy's Survival Guide

Dean Mignola

JDpress

Jackson Douglas Press

Published by
Jackson Douglas Press
P.O. Box 3196, Shell Beach, CA 93448

Cover design
Garth Turner

Illustrations
Jason Johnson

Interior design and layout
Encompas Printing & Graphics
www.encompas.net

Editing
A Writer's Eye

Library of Congress Control Number: 2004096636

ISBN: 0-9742011-0-3

Printed in the United States of America

Acknowledgments

I must first thank my college and post-college roommates and friends because it's our struggles to survive single life that inspired this book. I would also like to thank the hundreds of women who shared insight into the mystery of what drives them and what they really want in a man. I've never met Dr. David Buss but I must thank him for sharing his and others' research on the strategies of human mating. It's this research that laid the foundation for the advice in this book. I can't neglect to thank my lovely bride Lisa, who supported me throughout the process and who gently encouraged me saying, "Finish that damn book, already!" I would also like to thank David Ruprecht for helping me keep the writing light and lively and Darlene Snodgrass, Jessica Kueffer and Josh Pruett for donating their editing skills and suggestions early in the process. A special thanks goes out to my good friend Matt Dathe for helping me through the design and printing stages. Finally, I would like to thank my proofreaders Miranda Battenburg and Susan and Editor Kevin Quirk, M.A. of A Writer's Eye. Kevin told me the book needed a consistent guiding hand and then proceeded to provide that guiding hand with incredible skill and talent.

CONTENTS

Chapter 1

WHY WOULD I NEED A SURVIVAL GUIDE?

SINGLE GUYS NEED A SURVIVAL GUIDE

One of my college roommates never learned how to cook. Let's call him Jeff since that's his name. When Jeff and I first moved away to college, he subsisted on cold cereal and peanut butter sandwiches. One day Jeff and I and our other roommates were going through a grocery store checkout lane when Jeff abruptly tossed something on the checkout counter. The checker and all four roommates stared at the item for a few seconds. Then everyone, except Jeff, exploded into a solid minute of gut-wrenching laughter. On the counter was an extra large tube of Preparation H. The poor guy couldn't cook a healthy meal to save his hemorrhoid-ravaged ass.

You may have a friend who pulls his laundry out of the wash severely wrinkled and permanently faded to a pinkish gray hue. Maybe you know a guy whose breath could knock a buzzard off a shit wagon. You might even know a guy whose idea of a meaningful relationship is a two-for-one lap dance at the Spearmint Rhino. Is it possible that you know a guy like this...from the inside?

Let's face it. Most guys need help with surviving life as a single guy. We eagerly, strenuously, obsessively master skills necessary for activities such as basketball and business. Rarely do we bone up on how to become a babe-magnet bachelor. The lucky guys get a couple of tips on clothes and cooking from Mom or pick up a few grooming pointers from Dad or a big brother. Unfortunately, most other guys get little or incorrect help on these subjects, and rarely do guys get meaningful guidance in the important quest of meeting women.

The Trouble with Trial and Error

I've watched many of my friends struggle with single life. Some get by on trial and way too much error. It's a painful process to watch. Other guys marry the first girl who doesn't take out a restraining order so they can avoid being so pathetically alone.

That is unfortunate when you consider most men need nothing more than a grownup version of the Cub Scout Handbook. At a young age that book showed me how to properly handle a knife and how to make a fire. These were important skills I used to create much havoc and bedlam. Later in life it became painfully clear that young and not so young single guys, along with recently divorced guys, also need a how-to guide. The only difference is that today we need to know how to properly handle a woman and how to start a bonfire in her loins.

The Rewards are Sweet...and Sexy

Let's face it. Meeting beautiful women is a top priority for most single guys. For some it becomes an obsession. It sure was one for me. I used to wonder how some guys surrounded themselves with beautiful women while others got shot down like ducks during hunting season. Being a budding journalist, I decided to research the subject until I learned "THE SECRET." I read dozens of books, research studies and magazine articles and interviewed hundreds of beautiful women (work, work, work). I also talked to dozens of men whom I consider "Masters of the Game." I then started applying what I learned until I was able attract more than my share of beautiful women. Meeting women became a fun game that I knew I could win. Beautiful women began stuffing their phone numbers in my pocket and inviting me back to their place. Guys started calling me the "ultimate wingman" and I still get lots of invitations to go bar hopping because guys know I can help them "hook up" with beautiful women. No, I'm not some super stud. I'm about as average as they come. That's why I'm so confident that I can help you. I figured out what women really want in a man and what I didn't have I learned to fake. I eventually met a keeper (in a bar), married her (in a church) and sired a son (in the back seat of my BMW). She has filled my life with all the fun, good times, and great sex I can handle.

Now officially "off the market," I couldn't let this hard earned knowledge go to waste, so I packed everything I learned into The Single Guy's Survival Guide. As you read it, you'll get a step-by-step system for successfully meeting and seducing beautiful women that I call the "Ultimate Pick-up Strategy." You'll learn exactly what to say and how to say it to get the best possible response. Of course, that's just a piece of the pick-up puzzle. Two guys can walk up to the same woman and say the exact same thing to her in the same way. The first guy she quickly blows off. The second guy she…do I have to draw you a picture? How does the second guy do it? You will learn there are seven qualities that, according to scientific research, attract more women than a two-for-one shoe sale at Bloomingdales. Project these Modern Alpha Male qualities and some beautiful women will actually come on to you. I know that sounds hard to believe, but it happens every day.

Seven Qualities of the Modern Alpha Male

Why do aging rock stars date supermodels? Because they can. Let's face facts. Men are wired with a powerful attraction to youth and beauty and supermodels represent the ultimate of both those qualities.

Given the choice without consequence, most men would prefer to be with as many young and beautiful women as possible. Don't be too hard on yourself. We can't help it. It's in our genes and stems from many generations of genetic programming. Youth and beauty are strong indicators of health and fertility. Early prehistoric men who were able to mate with numerous young and beautiful women had a better chance of spawning numerous healthy children, thus increasing their chances of passing on their genetic makeup which, by the way, included the male preference to mate with a variety of young and beautiful women. That doesn't mean a man can't choose to focus on other qualities in a woman (yeah, right!). It just means those primal drives are real and we need to understand their potency.

Professor David Buss, in his book, *The Evolution of Desire*, analyzed the results of hundreds of research studies about the qualities people seek in the opposite sex. For example, studies of men from 37 different cultures were surveyed regarding what they look for in a mate. On average, they expressed a desire for wives approximately 2.5 years younger than themselves. The same research found that men in all 37 cultures valued physical appearance in a mate more than women did. This leads us to look at the other side of the relationship between rock stars and supermodels. Why do supermodels date aging rock stars? The answer once again lies in genetic survival.

While early man could attempt to hump every female in sight... and probably did, early woman risked nine months of pregnancy, the added obligation of raising a child and a sore scalp from being dragged around by her hair. To ensure that her genes would survive, she needed a mate who could provide resources and protection while sharing the obligation of raising their offspring. That makes the woman's job of looking for a mate much more complicated than a man's. She will consciously and unconsciously seek men who exhibit survival-enhancing characteristics hardwired into her genetic makeup over many generations. Rock stars in our society tend to be ambitious risk takers with a lot of wealth, power and status. These are four of the most important survival-related qualities women seek. The attraction to these qualities is so strong that some women beg rock stars to finger their neck, tune their strings and play them like a cherished Fender Stratocaster. It's the same way in the animal kingdom. In a variety of animal species a dominant male, or alpha male, gets to mate with his choice of females. Such dominance is often determined through fighting. However, coloring, mating dances, and mating calls are also used by certain male critters to attract female critters. The goal of these mating displays is to convince the female that this superior male will help her produce superior offspring, thus enhancing the survivability of her genes, not to mention provide adequate digs and grub.

Human females look for specific characteristics in a mate. I call these characteristics the Seven Qualities of the Modern Alpha Male. If you want to attract more women, you must develop the qualities that women are genetically programmed to seek in a man. In other words, before you can get into her jeans, you need to understand and appeal to her genes. As we saw with the example of rock stars, superior development of just a few of these characteristics can turn a pale, scrawny, androgynous screamer into a super babe magnet. As an added bonus, you will find that acquiring these qualities will help you succeed in just about every aspect of your life. So what are these mysterious qualities? They won't come as a big surprise. The Seven Qualities of the Modern Alpha Male are:

- Wealth
- Status
- Physical superiority
- Brains
- Ambition
- Commitment
- Compatibility

Makes sense, doesn't it? The trick is how you display these qualities to the women you meet.

Alpha Male Quality #1—Wealth

Our old friend Professor Buss cited surveys of people in America and all over the world that found that women value financial resources in a mate "roughly twice as much as men do." That means if you are a rich rock star, it's easier for you to attract supermodels. Um, how many of you are rock stars? That's what I thought. The rest of us can increase our attractiveness to women by learning how to create the appearance of wealth while we work to build some real wealth of our own. Chapter 2: Wealth—Multiply Your Money, will give you some valuable money-saving tips and get you started on attracting more money into your life. We'll also share a powerful technique for spending a little money to make a big impression.

Alpha Male Quality #2—Status

Women instinctively know that men with status and power have the ability to acquire resources that could benefit the survival of her and her children. Former Secretary of State Henry Kissinger is quoted as saying that power is the ultimate aphrodisiac. How else could a paunchy, myopic guy who sounded like a Viennese Yoda attract more than his share of beautiful babes? Our randy former President Bill Clinton would, no doubt, agree with Kissinger's assessment of status and its effect on women. I never understood why President Clinton used Monica as his oval orifice when he could have used his power and charisma to attract a much hotter woman. It may have something to do with the way she smoked his cigar. No doubt she was just one of several young ladies in his special internship program. In Chapter 3: Status—Don't Get Pecked in the Pecking Order, we'll show you how to display the image and symbols of status so you'll never have to settle for some pudgy girl in a blue dress.

Alpha Male Quality #3—Physical Superiority

American women prefer taller men, at least 5'11" tall. Who says? A study listed in Physical Appearance and Gender Sociobiology and Sociocultural Perspectives, Albany State University of New York Press. Can you get any more official than that? Researchers theorize that a healthy, athletic and slender body is better suited for survival because men with this physique tend to be more agile both in and out of the sack. But we don't need any fancy studies to prove this. We see a preference for tall and fit men displayed almost everywhere we look. A study of business executives found that taller men get promotions faster and easier than their shorter competitors. The quarterback gets the prettiest girl, not the center. Of course, the quarterback spends much of his time with his face in the center's ass, so maybe it balances out. James Bond, Hollywood's manifestation of the Modern Alpha Male, is a tall, slender guy who can outsmart and outfight much bulkier men. He also got to play around with Pussy Galore, but I digress. Not particularly tall? Not to worry. In Chapter 4: Physical Superiority—Build a Better Body, we have some tips to make you look at least one inch taller while enhancing the other physical qualities women lust after.

Alpha Male Quality #4—Brains

Mental ability can be just as important as physical prowess for the Modern Alpha Male. Women covet a superior brain because intelligence and "street smarts" can help a man acquire important advantages such as wealth, status and power. Women also hope to pass along this important trait to their children. Sorry, we can't work miracles in this department. But Chapter 5: Brains -Your Mind Is a Terrible Thing to Waste, will give you a technique for maximizing your memory and help you act smart, which is really half the battle, isn't it?

Alpha Male Quality #5—Ambition

Women realize the drive to succeed is one of the most important characteristics in determining whether a man will acquire and keep the coveted characteristics of money, power and status. In Chapter 6: Ambition -Scoring with Goals, you'll learn an amazing system for kicking yourself in the butt and getting what you want. You'll also learn to look ambitious even if, when you're alone, you're a lazy bum who can barely drag his hairy butt off the couch to get another beer.

Alpha Male Quality #6—Commitment

Throughout history, women have sought committed and dependable men to provide protection and resources to help them raise their children. This may seem less important today because of the job opportunities available to women, but it still holds true. You may not be ready to settle down and have kids. But you should know that most women are looking for clues that you are a dependable man who honors commitment. This can be faked! In Chapter 7: Commitment—How

Good Guys Finish First, you'll learn the power of a promise kept and how to refine your nice guy tendencies into a powerful tool for seducing women.

Alpha Male Quality #7—Compatibility

People of both sexes seek mates with similar values, interests and personalities. Research has shown that mismatched couples tend to break up more than those who are more alike. A good match also makes it easier to pursue mutual goals such as having children, extended family relations and successful social interactions. In Chapter 8: Compatibility—Creating the Connection, we'll share some amazing techniques for instantly building rapport with the women you meet. Even if you share only a few common interests, she'll feel like the two of you belong together. If you've ever heard a beautiful woman say, "You're just not my type," you'll want to check out this chapter and dump that problem for good.

The Alpha Male Scale

Uh-oh. Feeling just a bit Alpha-challenged in a couple of the seven qualities? Not to worry. You are far from alone. Only a small percentage of men are dominant in all of the seven qualities of the Modern Alpha Male. Those true Alpha Males can effortlessly enjoy their pick of beautiful women. Fortunately, you can do quite well simply by minimizing your weaknesses and focusing on one or two Modern Alpha Male qualities for which you already show promise. Take a few minutes to conduct a personal survey. This is not some "chat room" conversation where you lie to make yourself sound good. This survey is for your benefit only, so it's important to be as honest as possible.

Rank yourself on the following statements:

1 strongly disagree

2 mostly disagree

3 neutral

4 mostly agree

5 strongly agree

 # 1: Wealth

I get a lot done in a short amount of time.

1 2 3 4 5

I have more money than most people my age in my community.

1 2 3 4 5

Money flows to me more than it flows away from me.

1 2 3 4 5

I'm good at finding bargains.

1 2 3 4 5

#2: Status

In my social group I am considered a leader.

1 2 3 4 5

I keep my room neat and I am considered a sharp dresser.

1 2 3 4 5

I stand up for myself when challenged.

1 2 3 4 5

Most people would consider me confident.

1 2 3 4 5

#3: Physical

I am taller than most guys in my age group.

1 2 3 4 5

I am stronger/more athletic than most guys in my age group.

1 2 3 4 5

I exercise vigorously at least 3 hours a week.

1 2 3 4 5

I have excellent physical and oral hygiene.

1 2 3 4 5

#4: Mental

I am/was an above average student in school.

1 2 3 4 5

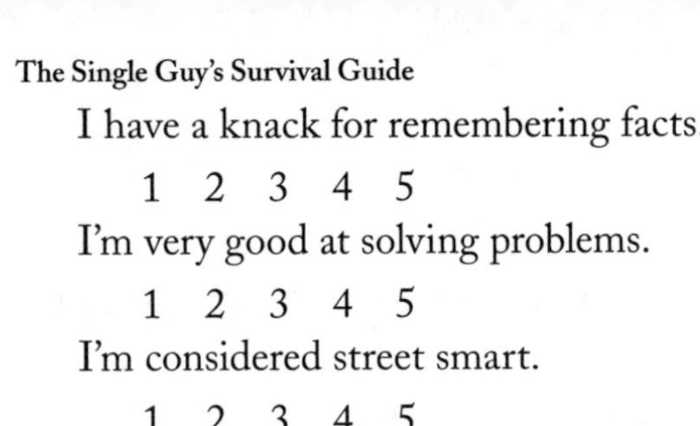

I have a knack for remembering facts.

1 2 3 4 5

I'm very good at solving problems.

1 2 3 4 5

I'm considered street smart.

1 2 3 4 5

#5: Ambition

I am very goal-oriented.

1 2 3 4 5

When I want something, I find a way to get it.

1 2 3 4 5

I am willing to work hard to get what I want.

1 2 3 4 5

I've written down my goals and a plan to achieve them.

1 2 3 4 5

#6: Commitment

I am dependable and am known for keeping my promises.

1 2 3 4 5

I am rarely late.

1 2 3 4 5

I am considered an excellent listener.

1 2 3 4 5

I am known as a "giver" in relationships.

1 2 3 4 5

#7: Compatibility

I am good at finding common interests with others.

1 2 3 4 5

I am considered congenial and likable.

1 2 3 4 5

I get along well with a variety of women.

1 2 3 4 5

The average person would not consider my beliefs to be extreme.

1 2 3 4 5

Now add up your ranking for each section. Write down the title of the two sections in which you scored the most points starting with the highest score first.

You are already kicking butt in these areas. Now write down the title of the two sections in which you had the lowest score with the lowest score first.

These are obviously the areas where your sorry ass needs help. You will get the best results if you accentuate the two areas that are your greatest strengths while learning how to minimize and/or improve your areas of weakness.

How do you rank on the Modern Alpha Male Scale?

Total up all your scores.

112+: You are a Modern Alpha Male...or you are lying to yourself as much as everyone else. You are successful and you find it relatively easy to meet and attract women. You'll be best served by skimming through much of The Single Guy's Survival Guide and picking out the priceless tactics and strategies that will make you unstoppable. Then again, it might be best to skim slowly; just in case you really were lying and can catch yourself before it's too late!

83-111: Like most guys, you currently play on the B Team. You've had some success with women but even a blind squirrel can find his nuts now and then. Turn to the chapters that cover your two greatest strengths and see how you can enhance these qualities even further. You'll also want to study the sections where you've identified your two weakest areas. Then read the rest of the book. You will be surprised how a few minor adjustments can make a world of difference in your life and your ability to attract women.

If your score is 82 or less, then you picked up The Single Guy's Survival Guide just in time! Apparently your stash of hand-and-body lotion sees more action than your condom cachet. Read through this whole book once and then reread the sections covering your two areas of greatest strengths and weaknesses. You will want to refer to the book as needed until the information and strategies sink in and become a part of you. Apply the techniques you learn and you will be thrilled with the results. This is not difficult, men! A little brainwork and determination, and the joys of The Modern Alpha Male are yours.

Chapter 2

HE DOESN'T LOOK LIKE MUCH, BUT HE SURE BRINGS HOME THE BACON.

WEALTH—MULTIPLY YOUR MONEY

It all started back in the cave days when the fearless caveman brought back dinner. You can almost hear the cave babes saying, "It's just as easy to fall in love with a good hunter." Some guys think it's shallow for a woman to be more attracted to a rich man than a poor one. Oh, right. As if guys show how deep *we* are when we focus on bra size over brain size! In fact, far from being shallow, a woman's attraction to wealth is a deeply-rooted part of her genetic programming. That programming is probably stronger if she's a successful executive herself. A wealthy man has the resources to make sure his mate and offspring get the best food, shelter and healthcare. A woman instinctively knows these advantages will benefit the survival of herself, her children, and her genes. She also knows that it usually takes other positive Alpha Male qualities to acquire wealth. Unless you were born with a silver spoon in your mouth, you will need time and effort to gain wealth. Fortunately, you don't have to be rich to reap wealthy benefits with women.

The Grand Gesture

This subject really makes some women pissed because they think it makes them sound money-grubbing. Well, if the Donna Karen pumps fit…just kidding…sort of. The truth is that most women don't expect you to be rich today. However, whether they admit it or not, women do look for signs of financial stability, generosity and your potential to roll in future greenbacks.

Let's tackle generosity first. You'll score major points if you show an interest in purchasing quality items and demonstrate a willingness to share what you have with her. This probably doesn't include sharing your Lakers tickets unless she enjoys watching really tall guys run around in silk shorts. The way to score points for generosity is something I call The Grand Gesture. In a nutshell, The Grand Gesture involves spending money on a woman in a way that she finds especially thoughtful or impressive, such as buying her something extravagant or taking her somewhere especially elegant. Buying a woman a drink is no longer considered so "grand." A true grand gesture would be to buy a round of drinks for the woman's entire group of friends. Or, be more creative and buy her group an order of appetizers or desserts. Any numb-nuts can show up with flowers from the grocery store or buy one of those roses wrapped in a plastic tube. It's far better to buy her one exotic flower or even a nice bouquet from the florist.

Another excellent example of The Grand Gesture is to buy a quality bottle of wine with dinner instead of buying wine by the glass. Never buy wine by the glass if you are trying to impress a woman and never insist on finishing the bottle to get your money's worth. If she prefers mixed drinks, ask which brand of alcohol she enjoys in her drink. The quality of the alcohol is especially important if you are drinking a shot. The difference in cost is usually minuscule compared to the impression you'll make on her. A good woman will appreciate that you are careful with money. However, you never want to come across as cheap.

You'll be flagged as a cheapskate if you do any of the following:

1. Complain about prices
2. Refuse to tip appropriately
3. Fail to buy refreshments at the movies or theater
4. Drive a junky car
5. Get a bad haircut
6. Wear shoddy shoes or clothes

Avoid these mistakes and reward a woman with a grand gesture on occasion and you'll be surprised at how positively she responds.

WARNING FLAG

Don't take your grand gesturing too far. It's important not to overwhelm a woman with gifts early in the relationship so she feels uncomfortably spoiled or obligated to you. Remember that you are not buying her time or sexual favors. That attitude will create the opposite effect you want. A grand gesture should be rare and given freely. The more casual you are about The Grand Gesture and the less you expect in return, the more she'll tend to show her appreciation in ways that you'll really appreciate.

The Wealthy Mindset

A fool and his money were lucky to get together in the first place.

– Harry Anderson

Big bucks don't just fall into your lap unless you are a lap dancer. Wealth starts with a mindset. Wealthy men look at money very differently from the average guy. The average man spends his money on frivolous items as soon as he gets his paycheck and then wastes even more of his money on credit card interest payments. Wealthy men know to PAY THEMSELVES FIRST by saving and investing at least 10% of their income as soon as they get it. Wealthy men avoid consumer debt at all costs because they know all that debt costs them big time down the road. By paying themselves first and avoiding consumer debt, these wealth-focused men can relax knowing exactly how much they can spend in a given month.

Go into an average guy's home and you will often find it a cluttered mess. There will be knickknacks on tables and worthless items crammed into every closet and drawer. Do you think there's a chance the guy's mind is equally cluttered? Because the furniture is cheap and abused, it must be replaced every few years. Now, go into a wealthy man's house. You will find his possessions are carefully selected and organized with care. There are fewer pieces of furniture per square foot of living space and some pieces may have been in the family for generations. The newer items are made of such high quality that it will last for generations. Often, wealthy men don't have significantly more stuff. They have better stuff and much of their "stuff" is actually real estate or business assets that create money for them.

Poor men waste their money on cheap clothes, big toys, knickknacks and lottery tickets that often become worthless the moment they leave the store. These impulse purchases usually require the guy to make other purchases in a chain reaction of spending. If you buy a fishing boat, the price of the boat is just the beginning of your expenditures. You will also need to register the boat, put gas in the boat, maintain the boat, store the boat, etc. The list goes on and on. When a wealthy man buys a boat, the cost is usually a small percentage of his net worth. He may invite business associates to the boat for parties or meetings and write the costs off as business expenses. Wealthy men spend most of their money on property, businesses and other investments that grow in value. If they do buy a consumer item, the money usually comes from the income generated from one of their investments. In other words, don't buy the Porsche today. Buy the property first and let the income pay for your Porsche down the road. The average guy rents his home while the wealthy man owns rentals.

I truly believe in the old saying that if you took away all the money from the wealthy and gave everyone an equal share, virtually all of the wealthy people would soon become wealthy again while the poor would squander their newly-found money in a matter of months or even weeks. Do you cram your money into your wallet or your pockets? Do you tend to rush and feel uncomfortable when you pay for something? This behavior identifies a common disregard and discomfort that many people have with money. I'll be straight with you. I have a nice beach house and drive a German luxury car, but I'm no millionaire—yet. I'm also not a financial expert, so use these investment suggestions I am about to offer to you solely as a springboard from which to do more research before you risk any of your own greenbacks.

One thing I can say with authority is that if you want more money in your life you need to dump the negative feelings you have about money. A dollar is not evil. It's simply a piece of paper that is worth what we all say it's worth. It's stupid to worship money and even worse to fear it. If you want to attract wealth into your life, show respect for money as a symbol of value and believe that you deserve to have money. My good friend Matt came from a well-to-do family and taught me two powerful principles that have many applications for attracting and keeping money in your life: "Never buy what you can get for free" and "Rarely pay retail."

Never Buy What You Can Get for Free

Matt and I both lived in Palm Springs, California for a while after college and we were pretty broke at the time. Whenever I pulled out my wallet to pay for something he would laugh and say, "Never buy what you can get for free." I noticed that I was spending a lot more money than he was and I finally asked him to put his mouth where his money was. Instead of telling me his money secrets he proceeded to show me. That day we sneaked into the swimming pool area at one of the nicest resort hotels in town. When we were asked our room number, Matt simply made one up. We weren't staying at the hotel, but we got all the perks and access to dozens of beautiful women who were lounging out by the pool. Matt joked with the bartender and flirted with the cocktail waitress and it wasn't long before we were being served complimentary drinks. Over the next few days we found some great Happy Hour spots and we gorged ourselves on free food at least three times a week. We would buy one drink each, tip generously and help ourselves to a buffet of food and bar babes.

I learned there are lots of ways to get what you want for free (not counting women). You can check the library before buying a book and check out the free entertainment newspapers for free community events. If a wine or beer festival is coming to town, offer to volunteer at one of the testing booths. My policy at a testing booth is "one for you and one for me." Women get friendly as they get loopy at those festivals, and they are especially friendly with the guys pouring them drinks. One of my favorite money-saving techniques is to type in the words "free stuff" on Google or Yahoo. You'll be surprised at how much cool stuff you can get for little or no money on the Internet. It's definitely a great way to buy magazine subscriptions. You can often get a year's subscription of your favorite magazine for free or for the price of one magazine on the news rack. Whenever you start to pull out your wallet, ask yourself "Is there some way I can get this for free or pay less?"

Rarely Pay Retail

Sometimes you have to pay. But you would be surprised to know how many local businesses give discounts to their best customers. Many times it's simply a matter of making friends with the owner or manager of the local store you frequent and nicely insisting on a discount. Clothing is generally marked up at least 100%. Jewelry can be marked up 400% or more. Many businesses routinely discount 10-50% on sale merchandise and still make a profit. You provide value to the business by your loyal patronage and by recommending the business to your friends and relatives. It's simply good business to reward loyal customers who bring their friends through the door. Most business owners and managers ask for discounts from their vendors; they'll respect you more for showing your guts and savvy when it comes to saving a buck.

It's a fact that wealthy men negotiate, and almost everything is negotiable. It helps to know how to do it effectively. By the way, with minor adjustments, you may find these rules also help when negotiating with potential lust-interests.

Seven Time-tested Rules of Negotiation:

1. Information is power. Know everything you can about the other party or parties in the negotiation. It's especially important to know what is being offered and what the other party wants most from the deal.
2. Ask with confidence for more than you expect but don't make the offer outrageous or you won't be taken seriously.
3. After you make your first offer, shut up and relax. Successful negotiators use silence as a powerful tool to subtly intimidate the other party into "caving."
4. Never give a concession without getting one from the other party. This is such a common tactic that shrewd negotiators expect it. It's called "the take away" because you take away something for everything you give up.
5. Make your second offer close to your first offer. The second offer sets the bar for the rest of the negotiation. A small concession shows the other party that you are serious about negotiating yet close to your "limit." Never agree to "split the difference." If the other party is willing to go halfway, he is usually willing to go even further.
6. Look for win-win solutions to help close the deal. This is where knowing what the other person wants comes into play. Show the other person how he can get what he wants while helping you get what you want.
7. Never gloat when you feel you have the upper hand in a negotiation. A win-lose mentality can give you a bad reputation that will hurt future negotiations with the other party and any of his friends and associates.

More Ideas for Saving Money

Entertain "in"—Dinner and drinks for two people at an average restaurant can cost $50 to $100 or more. At home, you can serve a nice dinner and drinks for a fraction of that amount. You also benefit from the added advantage of proximity to your bedroom. No doubt the best place for dessert. Dinner at your place is a little ballsy for a first date, but it ain't a bad second date if the two of you are hitting it off.

You'll save money and your health if you shop along the perimeter of the grocery store and avoid the center aisles. The processed and frozen foods found in those center aisles cost more and often contain saturated fat, artificial preservatives and flavor enhancers that will harm your health and your waistline over time.

Exception: frozen vegetables. Usually, vegetables are frozen soon after they are freshly picked so they maintain many of their nutrients. Vegetables in your produce aisle may have been picked prematurely so they don't spoil during shipping or on the shelf. Frozen vegetables will also last a lot longer in your freezer compared to fresh vegetables that often quickly grow limp in the refrigerator. As we all know, there is only one thing worse than a limp vegetable.

Your savings will really add up if you pay attention to price per ounce or pound when buying food. Sometimes the bigger packages are not the best value. This is especially true if half of the food spoils into a greenish-gray mass because you couldn't eat it all at one sitting. You might want to experiment with generic and store brand foods. Often they are the same items distributed by higher-priced brand name companies at around half the price. Try purchasing generic brands of grocery items that you buy on a regular basis. If there doesn't seem to be a difference, buy the generic version so you can save the difference. I know, this may seem like a contradiction to my advice about buying quality. However, while quality is important for items and services wherein the difference is evident (clothes, cars, wine), when the quality is comparable, shop by price.

Increase your insurance deductibles - Increasing your auto insurance deductible to $500 can reduce your comprehensive and collision premiums by up to 30%. You should only use your insurance for serious accidents anyway. The insurance companies will often up your premium or dump you if you use your insurance more than once in a year or two. Rental car insurance is usually a waste if you are already well covered under your regular car insurance or even your credit card. Check with your insurance agent to make sure you aren't paying twice for the same insurance when you rent a car. Those rental car companies make much of their profit selling insurance to people who don't need it. O.K., I bet you're starting to think, "What does insurance have to do with meeting chicks?" Not much. I'm just trying to save you some money so you can afford to take those chicks out. I'll keep the money-saving tips brief so we can jump to the meat of attracting and meeting women.

Refuse to pay for extended warranties on appliances and electronics. They are almost pure profit for the store and generally a rip-off for the consumer. If the product is so unreliable that it needs an extended warranty, you probably don't want it.

Shop for better telephone rates. Competition is hot in the cell phone and wired phone service industry. Many people are paying more than double what they should for phone service just because they are too lazy to pick up the phone and ask a few questions. While we're at it, isn't it about time you cut back on those calls to 1-900-hot teens?

Purchase airline tickets and hotel rooms online to save 10-40% on travel expenses. Exception: for complicated travel plans it's worthwhile to use a travel agent. They handle the details and it's usually worth the small extra expense.

Hold a garage/yard sale. Get rid of all the stuff you don't need and save the money you make. Price your stuff at about half what you think it's worth. It'll move out quickly and you'll save yourself the trouble of having to move a bunch of crap back into your garage. Even a couple hundred dollars invested properly can turn into thousands in a few short years.

Probably the most important money-saving tip is to pay off your car loan and credit cards and switch to one low-interest credit card or, even better, a debit card. It's amazing how many people are paying as much as 18-21% on a pile of store credit cards when it's so easy to find a VISA or Mastercard with rates as low as 9% or less. When the card company starts to increase your interest rate, simply switch cards.

WARNING FLAG

Only switch credit cards when necessary to get a lower rate. Too much card switching can hurt your credit rating.

Of course, the best approach is to pay off your credit card as soon as possible and use a debit card when cash or a check is not appropriate. A debit card works just like a credit card but there is no interest charge because you are simply removing money from your checking account. If you do nothing else to improve your financial future, tear up your credit cards and work out a plan to pay off all consumer debt as soon as possible. The thousands of dollars you save on interest payments each year will allow you to buy better stuff in the long run.

Investing Mistakes to Avoid

Raw land: Undeveloped land creates no income. Sometimes it's sold at inflated rates with creative financing. Leave land deals to the experts.

Time-Shares: Think of time-share as a girl you can only date two weeks a year, but you have to pay up front for all the dates you may or may not enjoy in the future. A time-share is usually a vacation property owned by multiple investors. Each investor gets access to the property for about one to two weeks a year. Good investments go up in value. Time-shares almost always go down in value. Time-shares also hold hidden costs such as maintenance fees, and there is always the chance the time-share company will go bankrupt. You may have seen TV commercials promising fast cash for time-shares. You can bet those companies are offering a few pennies on the dollar compared to what the owner originally paid. No matter how good the sales pitch, don't get talked into a time-share.

Individual Stocks: For the less-experienced investor, buying individual stocks is riskier than investing in mutual funds because you get less diversification. It's kind of like women. Play the field until you really know what you are looking for. However, if you are willing to invest the time to study the habits and advice of the best investors, individual stocks can be a great way to invest your money.

Bonds and Bond Mutual Funds: Over time, bonds under perform stocks and actively traded bond funds often carry high expenses. I'm sure professional bond traders could argue this point and if you really know the bond market you can push the odds in your favor. However, for the average guy, I think there are better options.

Invest with the Best

If you want to be a wealthy guy, you have to start acting like one today. Always pay yourself 10% first: Most guys live paycheck to paycheck. They get a raise and they still live paycheck to paycheck. When it comes time to retire they've bought lots of stuff they didn't need and they live in relative poverty because they have little or no money outside of what they get from Social Security. If you want to trust the Federal Government to finance your future, I've got some prime oceanfront property in Arizona I'd like to sell you. Starting next paycheck, take 10% right off the top. At first the 10% should go to pay off your consumer debt such as credit cards. Start with the card with the highest interest rate and pay off the cards one at a time so you get a sense of accomplishment each time you pay off a card. As soon as you pay off your consumer debt, start putting that 10% into some kind of investment for your savings and retirement. If your employer offers a 401K or 403B (income tax shelters) you may be able to have the money directly withheld from your paycheck and automatically deposited into a mutual fund. Otherwise, place the money in a separate savings account. With direct deposit you can probably have this done automatically. I'm a big fan of automatic investment plans, which take a prearranged amount of money from your bank account every month. In fact, if your employer offers matching funds to your retirement account, start investing the amount matched while you pay off your consumer credit.

I'm amazed at the number of young guys who don't participate in their employer-sponsored 401K savings plans at least up to the amount of the company's matching contribution. Matching funds in a tax sheltered investment account is basically FREE MONEY that you should never pass up. Another great tax shelter is buying shares in a mutual fund in a Roth IRA. A Roth allows your after-tax money to accumulate without any taxation of the compound interest. A traditional IRA is usually the second-best choice. It shelters your pretax money today. But you will be taxed when you eventually take the money out.

Multiply Your Money in A Mutual Fund: Recent Wall Street scandals aside, when you buy a mutual fund you are in theory hiring an experienced team of traders to study the market and buy investments for you at very little cost. This doesn't protect you from market dips. Many stock mutual funds lost 20-50% through 2001 and 2002. However, a diversified mutual fund will diminish the impact of price swings compared to individual stocks and bonds. Most mutual funds are also liquid, which means you can take your money out when needed. The exception is when your mutual fund is tax sheltered in a company retirement plan or IRA. Removing money from such sheltered funds can bring a big tax penalty. So hold off on the plasma TV until you have the cash in hand. However, you can usually move your money from one fund to another fund within the fund family without penalty.

Instead of buying mutual funds from a bank or a broker, knock out the high fees of the middle man by working directly with the mutual fund company. Vanguard is a mutual fund company that often gets praised by the experts because it offers no-load funds with very low fees. There are plenty of others to choose from. You can find toll-free numbers for these companies from any good financial magazine or newspaper. Just call the mutual fund company and tell them your situation and they will be happy to send you the appropriate forms and information to help guide you. Once you start the fund, you can have the money automatically transferred from your checking account into the mutual fund. You can also move your money from one fund to another within the same mutual fund family with little more than a phone call. There are funds that specialize in common stocks, others that invest in bonds, and some that invest in specific industries or use special investment strategies.

You can get ratings of mutual funds from a company called Morningstar. Most libraries have a copy of the Morningstar ratings behind the reference desk. Read a couple of books and magazine articles on picking mutual funds and narrow your search to funds that have been rated with four or five stars; then match the amount of risk you can tolerate. Don't you wish there was a rating system like this for women? "Babestar gives her four stars. When she goes down, you'll go up!" Guess we better get back to money. You'll get enough on sex in Chapter 12.

Generally, the longer you have to invest, the more risk you can take, as long as you are not the type to move your money the first time your investment shows a loss.

If all this sounds like too much hassle, consider starting with an index fund such as Vanguard's Index 500 or Vanguard's Total Market. These no-load stock funds seek to passively follow a broad range of stocks. The S&P 500 is a grouping of 500 of the biggest and (hopefully) most stable companies in the United States. The Total Market fund follows the total stock market, which includes a lot of smaller companies that have more room for growth. Both funds routinely beat about three-fourths of the stock mutual funds out there and they offer some of the lowest management fees and tax liabilities available. Most analysts agree that there is no evidence that "load funds" (where you pay a commission) perform better than "no-load" funds, so stick with the no-loads. Vanguard also offers some great bond index funds with super low fees. If you want to try adding bonds to your investment portfolio, this is a great way to go. Most guys under 50 will want most of their money in stock mutual funds with some cash in money market funds and some in index bond funds. The mutual fund companies will be happy to send you literature with suggestions on the right percentage of each to meet your circumstances and attitudes about risk.

Again, these suggestions are meant as an introduction to the world of investing. My goal is to help you avoid high risk and high cost investments. There are sharks out there who will try to talk you into letting them invest for you. Take the time to invest in your financial intelligence before you invest your money and you can avoid portfolio shark bite. Here is one final investment tip that is little more than a hunch. I'm going to move some of my money out of the stock market to other investments such as money market investments, CDs and property around the year 2010. That's when the Baby Boom generation will begin reaching retirement age. I'm betting that the stock market could take a plunge when this massive group of new retirees begins removing money from investments to pay for their leisure years.

Grow Rich with Rentals

When you rent, you are paying a mortgage for someone else. There are many creative ways to buy a home or rental property with little money down, and there are good books and audio programs to help you find and purchase the right investment properties. A good way for a single guy to get started is to buy a house and rent the extra rooms out to his friends. "Oh gee Tiffany, can't make the rent this month? I guess we could work something out." The goal is to get the combined rents to cover the mortgage and the property taxes. The principle payments and the appreciation on the property will build equity in the house that can be used to make a down payment on a second property.

There are four rules to follow when buying a rental property:

1. Pick a desirable location or a location that is poised to become desirable.
2. Find an owner who is eager to sell.
3. Pick a property in which the needed repairs are affordable to you.
4. Negotiate a low price on the property because you'll often make most of your money on the purchase rather than the sale of an investment property.

Obviously, this is just a brief introduction to the world of real estate investing. Some people prefer to buy properties to fix them up and sell them for a quick profit. Also, when you are buying investment property, use an agent who specializes and owns investment property so you can gain from that person's investment insight and experience.

Whichever way you plan to invest your money, read some good books on the subject and talk with people who have been successful investors before you risk your own money. Then go for it! Donald Trump doesn't attract all those gorgeous women up to his penthouse with his snooty personality and comb-over haircut.

Chapter 3

WHAT'S HE GOT THAT WE DON'T?
A PLATINUM RECORD

STATUS—DON'T GET PECKED IN THE PECKING ORDER

Women prefer a man who commands respect from those around him. Attractive women tend to avoid men who are submissive and easily dominated. This is the origin of the cliché "nice guys finish last." A woman wants to know that you will stand up for yourself and that you will protect her if necessary. It wouldn't hurt to take some classes in martial arts, self-defense or boxing. The confidence, discipline and physical fitness you gain will be well worth the effort.

She'll also look for a sense of confidence in your eyes and the way you carry yourself. A woman who doubts your assertiveness may test you by teasing you or insulting you with verbal jabs to see if you have the confidence to defend yourself. Don't be afraid to dish it back in a playful manner and never pine after a woman like a lovesick puppy dog unless you want to remain forever in the "just friends" category.

Fake It Until You Make It

Confidence is a powerful way to project high status. True confidence is hard to fake, but you'll find a little practice helps. When I first met Tim he was short on cash as well as stature but never short on the company of beautiful women. I was a bit shy back then and I was amazed at his ability to attract a crowd of women who seemed to follow him and hang on his every word. We became good friends and, after persistent questioning, I finally got Tim to spill his secret.

Tim revealed that he was fascinated by the ability of some actors to alter the way they presented themselves. An actor might play a geek for one movie and a successful stud for another. Tim also noticed that the actor could appear confident on screen and insecure outside of the role. He thought it strange that all actors didn't "act" confident all the time. Tim told me one day he decided to star in his own movie with the whole world as his supporting cast and audience. For this role, he chose to study and adopt the posture, mannerisms, facial expressions and speaking style of the movie stars he so admired. He practiced standing with his head and shoulders back and flashing a confident smile as though he was walking down the red carpet at the Academy Awards. He tried strutting slightly when he walked and spoke with passion and plenty of eye contact. He even dressed the part, wearing only expensive brands of clothing and maintaining them impeccably. No one noticed that he wore the same four shirts and two pairs of pants over and over again.

Tim told me that when he started feeling nervous or insecure he would picture how a movie star like Tom Cruise would act in the same situation. He would also repeat over and over that he was the best looking guy in the room and that all the women wanted to meet him. At that point I thought Tim was nuts. But I couldn't argue with his results.

Eventually Tim convinced me to try his technique for myself. I found it unnatural and awkward at first. But I soon learned that the approach had hidden benefits. I found from personal experience that our emotions are somewhat influenced by how we move our bodies and what we focus on in our minds. When I stood up straight with a big smile on my face and focused on positive thoughts, I eventually began to feel more confident. According to research on the subject, your subconscious mind has trouble determining the difference between "reality" and thoughts that are reinforced with emotion and repetition. If you enthusiastically tell yourself phrases like "I'm a winner," "I've got this under control," "I've got what it takes," while standing tall and picturing yourself successful, your subconscious mind eventually accepts it as fact.

The right questions can be just as empowering. Try asking yourself questions such as, "How would a totally confident person act in this situation?" or "How can I feel great about myself right now?" Some people think it's unnatural to use positive visualization, questioning and self-talk. But the best athletes and top executives do it every day to give them an edge. In fact, many of these Modern Alpha Males believe the real difference between champions and would-be champions is the ability to consistently pump positive images and thoughts into their minds during critical moments. Repetition and emotion are the key elements that make this work. So what have you got to lose? Repeat these images and phrases/questions often and make them as vivid as possible.

There are two superior times for visualization and self-talk. The first is when you are about to go to sleep. This allows the words and images to cycle around in your subconscious while you are sleeping. Eventually, you'll find you have more control over your dreams and that they will become more positive and enjoyable. Another great time for visualization and self-talk is right before you engage in the critical activity. See yourself performing the activity flawlessly and picture yourself celebrating your success. Tell yourself what a great job you are doing over and over again with passion and emotion. This process won't work just by reading about it. If you want to get better results, put it into practice.

Become a Big Fish

In high school, my brother had a friend named Taylor who was smart and outgoing but a little too small and quirky to attract the A-list girls. Taylor became frustrated with his lack of attractive female prospects and noticed a clique at the school that included some beautiful girls that most guys overlooked. These girls were decked out in black clothes, strangely colored hair and wild makeup. Taylor didn't have a "gothic" bone in his body. But it wasn't long before he started conforming to this group of "non-conformists" by wearing eyeliner and similar clothes. He quickly became one of the leaders of this clique, and you wouldn't believe the wild things he got those girls to do with him and each other! Status is a relative thing. If you feel like a small fish, you can always look for a smaller pond.

Small Talk with the Little People

Men of status feel comfortable talking with just about anyone and they easily spark conversations wherever they go. If you are the strong-silent type or the not-so-strong shy type, it's a good idea to get some people practice. You probably come into contact with dozens of strangers a day. Test the water and dip into some quick conversations. Think of it as a warm-up before a big workout.

The weather is a safe topic. You can also talk about something the person is doing or wearing, or you can discuss something in your surroundings. You'll probably make some person's day and you just might get a reputation as a friendly guy. Don't dismiss small talk as a waste of time. The little old lady you meet in the grocery line may decide you are the perfect person to set up with her niece, the lonely swimsuit model. Once you get used to chatting with "the little people," you can move onto something more adventurous. Make it a point to say "hi" to women who seem totally out of your league. It's fun to play in the "big leagues" because you have nothing to lose. Offer a quick compliment, ask a quick question or two and move on. You'll be surprised how accessible and nice women can be when you act casually friendly toward them. You may find some of these women aren't as out of reach as you first thought. Most drop-dead beautiful women intimidate guys so much that they get approached by aggressive jerks or not at all.

If you find yourself getting star struck, use a variation of the old public speaker's trick. Public speakers sometimes make themselves less nervous by picturing their audience naked. Of course, you probably already do that with beautiful women and it no doubt has the opposite effect. This is no time to send your blood to the wrong head. Instead, picture her in an embarrassing situation like getting caught sitting on the toilet or smiling with a piece of parsley stuck between her teeth. The goal is to bring her down from the pedestal you built in your mind just long enough for you to interact with her in a casual manner. Beautiful women are just people who live with many of the same insecurities as everyone else. Trust me, even Cameron Diaz thinks she looks fat in certain outfits. Uh-oh, there you go again. Picturing Cameron Diaz naked is not going to help you relax around women. When you act casual and friendly, most women will react to you in kind. Any bartender will tell you that it's the friendly guys who leave with the most beautiful women.

Getting Help from the Guys

In college, some friends and I engaged in a bizarre but effective confidence building ritual before going out to meet women. Each guy would pay extra attention to his grooming and put on his "lucky shirt" or his "lucky underwear." For some guys, lucky meant the clothing had never yet experienced the stain of a woman's rejection. For the real players, it was simply an article of clothing the guy wore the last time he got lucky (hopefully it had been washed since). If one guy ran out of lucky shirts he'd borrow a shirt from another guy and it's newness made it instantly lucky. Of course, you never wore another guy's lucky underwear. That's just nasty. Inevitably, one guy would be primping more than the rest and that would start a round of semi-sarcastic compliments. A guy nearby would say, "You're going to have to fight off the women tonight." The guy doing the primping would respond with, "Coming from a great looking guy like you, that means a lot." Then someone else would pipe in with, "You guys are a couple of chick magnets, but I've got on my lucky underwear and they haven't failed me yet!" The compliments and boasts would get more and more outrageous and they continued at the bars and parties later that night.

You need to know that we are not talking about a bunch of chiseled and arrogant male models. These are regular looking, sports-playing, beer-drinking guys. Sure, the sarcasm ran thick. But this banter served to pump up our confidence level like a coach's pep talk before the big game. Those nights we laughed off the rejection of the occasional snooty coed. In our twisted minds we were a bunch of "chick magnets" wearing our "lucky underwear" and the girls we met were foolish to miss the party!

Symbols of Status

Women look for clues of your status. Remember, it's in their DNA. Stylish clothes, an expensive watch and a nice car are some of the most obvious status symbols. There are others as well. You don't want to go overboard or come across as a showoff. However, the subtle use of a couple of status symbols can help you maximize your success with women:

1. The Beautiful Female Friend: Years ago I took a night class at a local college and noticed a beautiful woman sitting in the classroom across from me. After the class I spotted the same young lady trying to politely avoid a guy who was harassing her for a ride home. I stepped up pretending to be her boyfriend and told the guy to move on. She was very thankful and we became fast friends. It turns out Jaimie was a former beauty queen and occasional model. Spending time with Jaimie taught me a lot about how beautiful women think and it helped me become much more comfortable around the kind of jarring beauty that intimidates most men.

Another benefit of having a beautiful female friend was that many women seemed to find me more attractive when I was with Jaimie. It turns out that a beautiful woman can be the ultimate status symbol. Women figure you must have something special going for you if you have a beautiful woman at your side. They also get to see how well you treat a woman. Since you are, in fact, still single, you can subtly pursue these interested women as long as you don't ignore your friend in the process. Love interests come and go. As I found with Jaimie, a good friendship can last for years. Nurture a friendship with at least one attractive female and you will find the relationship brings many benefits:

- She'll be a great source of advice on the opposite sex and clothes.
- She may set you up with some of her gorgeous friends! Beautiful women tend to travel in packs.
- She may get lonely and decide to jump your bones when you least expect it!

WARNING FLAG

While it is a good idea to have one or two female friends, you don't want to make a habit of being "just friends" with the women you meet. Some guys think that listening to a woman's problems and being her friend will make her want to sleep with them. Actually, the opposite is true. Once you fall into the therapist or friend category with a woman it is hard to climb out. If you are attracted to a woman, don't go out of your way to listen to all her problems or be her buddy. Show interest in her and flirt with her right from the start and make sure you work to spark her sexual fire early and often.

2. High-Status Steel: Do you drive a racy sports car or a dull subcompact? Is your car clean and neat, or is it littered with fast food wrappers and reeking of body odor? The vehicle that you drive and how it's maintained speaks volumes about you to the women you date. Women pay more attention to automobile brands than the model year. As a general rule, a woman will be more impressed with an older high-status car that is well maintained compared to a newer, economy car. The specific model depends on your personality and resources as well as the type of woman you are trying to attract. Here are a few examples:

Mustang, Firebird and Camero—These American muscle cars are great for attracting that blue-collar babe with big hair who wears tight jeans and a pushup bra.

Jetta, Passat and Mini Cooper—Sporty imports like these are reliable, affordable and a great choice for that young sporty guy trying to attract an equally young and sporty girl.

Ford and GM trucks—Stay away from the small economy trucks and consider a crew cab or SUV for more interior room. The foxy farmer's daughter with her western shirt and Wrangler jeans will appreciate that you drive American metal just like her daddy. Oh, and a friendly Labrador or Golden Retriever in the truck bed will seal the deal. Don't waste your money on obscene lift kits and gargantuan tires. Most women assume that the size of your tires is inversely proportionate to the size of your unit.

Just about any BMW, Mercedes, Audi and Lexus—These German and Japanese luxury cars generally come loaded as "pre-owned" cars and tend to be pampered by the previous owners. Also, the makers of these cars are slow to change body designs. That means you can often find an older model luxury car in great shape. Just about any woman who appreciates the finer things will appreciate that you drive foreign luxury.

Porsche and Italian sports cars—These fast and high-maintenance lovelies attract women with the same qualities. You better have a six-figure income if you expect to drive in this fast lane.

Great cars that single guys may want to avoid—Civic (small), Miata and Volkswagen Bug (feminine), Camry, Accord, most American sedans, any mini-van and older Volvos (boring).

ISN'T THE MOTOR AT THE OTHER END?

Keep it Clean—How you maintain your car is often at least as important as the model you drive. Any car that is dirty, messy or odorous sends a clear message that you are a lazy slob. Ok, so maybe you are. Don't let her know that! Most women are happy to ride in an average car as long as it's clean and neat. Keeping your car clean and waxed also protects the finish from scratches and rust. Pay close attention to the interior to make sure it's neat, and clean and odor free.

HOT TIP

Don't hang one of those cardboard pine trees from your rear view mirror unless you want to broadcast to the world, "I stink." Instead, spray the carpets with fabric deodorizer at least once a month or grab one of those fabric softener sheets from your laundry supplies and tuck it under your car seat between the springs and the seat cushion.

Your car should not contain porn or any evidence of the other women you are dating. Which reminds me of the guy in the locker room whose buddy asks, "When did you start wearing women's panties?" To which the guy responds, "When my wife found a pair in my glove compartment." Your car should be stocked with romantic music, condoms (in a good hiding place) along with a blanket in the trunk. You don't have to be a Boy Scout to be prepared.

Keep it Rolling—Today's cars are sophisticated machines loaded with electronic equipment that requires extensive training to understand. If the motor doesn't turn it's probably the battery. If it turns but doesn't start it's either an ignition problem or it's not getting gas. A whining noise is usually a loose belt, which is usually easy to fix. Any grinding noise is usually bad news that will require the attention of a mechanic. You don't have to be mechanically inclined to maximize the life of your car and minimize repair bills if you follow some basic tips:

1. Find a good mechanic who specializes in your type of car and treat him like a king so he keeps an eye on little problems before they become big problems. Offering a $10 tip or a six-pack of beer can be money well spent.
2. Allow your car to warm up for 30 seconds EVERY TIME you start your car. Yes, it's just as important as foreplay and doesn't take nearly as long. This simple step will greatly lengthen the life of your car's motor because it allows it to warm and the oil

to circulate before you put too much strain on the engine.

3. Keep the air pressure at recommended levels in your tires and rotate your tires every 10,000 miles. These tire tips will make driving safer, extend the life of your tires and maximize fuel economy big time.
4. Keep fluids properly topped off.

Radiator: Many new cars have a reservoir near the radiator that is easy to check. There are little lines on the reservoir that say, "add" or "low" and "full." If your car has such a reservoir, you can add water. If the level is very low you'll probably want to add a combination of water and antifreeze as specified in your owner's manual and the antifreeze container. If your car does not have such a reservoir, you will need to remove the radiator cap. Use a rag and turn the cap very slowly because an overheated radiator may be under pressure to overflow. You'll have to work extra hard to meet women if you permanently scald your face with radiator steam. The liquid should be an inch or two from the top of the radiator. Just as with the reservoir, if you need just a little liquid, add water. If the radiator is very low it's best to add a combination of water and antifreeze.

Oil: The engine should be warm and turned off, and the car should be somewhat level when you check the oil. Pull out the dipstick from the engine block and wipe with a paper towel before inserting all the way back into its slot. I know you are expecting a sexual innuendo here, but it's just too easy. Pull the stick out again and add a quart of oil if the oil is at or below the "low" or "add" indicator. To add oil, unscrew the oil cap and use a funnel or spout to pour in the oil. Remember to screw the oil cap back on tightly and make sure you wipe up any oil that spills on the engine because excessive spill on the manifolds could catch fire. The "weight" of oil is its thickness. In cold weather you generally want a lower number for thinner oil. Your owner's manual should have suggestions, and 10-40 is a safe bet if you have to guess. Try not to mix oils of different weights when you can avoid it.

Everyone Needs a Jump-start

Sure, you could get the shock of your life or your battery could explode if you do it wrong. But jump-starting a car is easy if you follow some basic steps:

Position the running car so that its battery is near the battery of the dead car without the two cars touching and turn off both ignitions and all lights and accessories. Use one jumper cable to clip the positive (+) battery terminal from the live car to the positive (+) terminal of the dead car. Remember: Plus to plus will start the bus. Use the other jumper cable to clip the negative (-) battery terminal from the live car to a non-moving part of the chassis (engine block) or the negative battery terminal of the dead car. Start the engine of the live car and let it run at least 30 seconds before starting the dead car. Revving the engine of the live car provides an extra boost of power if the dead car initially fails to start. Remove the jumper cables in the reverse order that you clipped them on and drive the previously dead car for at least 30 minutes before turning off the engine.

Push-start—If you don't have jumper cables or another car, you may be able to push-start the car if you have a standard transmission and at least one strong friend (or a hill). One person gets behind the wheel while one or more people push (or you allow the car to coast down the hill). Put the car in second gear and disengage the brakes. When the car gets some momentum, pop the clutch and pump the gas slightly. Repeat if necessary and drive the car for at least 30 minutes before turning off the engine.

Don't Get Jacked Changing a Tire

There are two things to remember when you change a tire: 1. You are going to get dirty. 2. You should never get under the car when it's up on a jack. Carry a can of "Flat Fix" to avoid changing a tire on the road if possible. If a tire change is necessary, here are the correct steps to follow: Drive to level ground and engage the emergency brake and transmission. Pry the hubcap off with the flat end of your lug wrench, just as you would open a paint can. Loosen each lug nut slightly with the wrench by turning counter clockwise. Extend the jack so that it stands straight and attaches to the car at a solid point of the frame or bumper near the flat (usually indicated by a diagram on the jack and a notch or recess in the frame). Extend the jack until the tire is about an inch off the ground making sure the jack never tilts from vertical.

Remove the flat tire, put on the spare and put nuts back on finger-tight. Lower the jack so the wheel touches the ground and finish tightening the nuts in a cross pattern so that you are not tightening the nut next to the nut you just tightened to avoid warping the wheel. If you've ever had your nuts tightened, you know how bad that can be! Finish compressing the jack and put it back the way you found it.

The Perfect Parallel Park

This section has nothing to do with keeping your car running and everything to do with keeping your dignity while you try to park.

Find a parking spot at least four feet longer than your car and signal the traffic behind you by activating the brake lights and turn signal. Make sure no car is about to pass you because the front of your car will arc into the next lane. Pull up next to the forward car so that your back wheels are lined up and turn the steering wheel slowly to the right as you back slowly into the space. When your front wheels line up with the back wheels of the forward car, begin to straighten your wheels. When your front bumper is even with the rear bumper of the forward car, turn the steering wheel all the way to the left and continue backing in. Once your car is near the rear car, turn the wheel to the right as you move forward until you are parallel to the curb and centered in the space.

Now that you have a handle on maintaining and parking your status symbol on wheels, we can move onto another potential status symbol that provides the funding to make the other status symbols possible.

It's Not Just a Job

A couple of my friends love to make up Alpha Male careers when they pick up women. They usually claim to be astronauts or professional baseball players. Some women see through the ploy. But my friends have so much fun describing their challenges and accomplishments that most women enjoy playing along with the charade. "Exaggerating" during the pickup process is one of the oldest tricks in the book. It's so common that a lot of women laugh it off when they finally learn that the guy doesn't have one of those prestigious careers. At least she knows that he is creative, which is important in someday attaining a high-status job. The downside is that it can be difficult to get a woman to trust you long-term when some of the first words she hears peg you as a dirty rotten stinking no good liar.

A more honest approach is to put a positive spin on the job you actually have. There are many ways to make your profession sound more interesting than the actual job title. A woman wants to be proud of the man she's with. Give your job a brief positive spin to help her feel good about being with you. Then you can shift the focus of the conversation toward talking about her and her interests.

Here are some examples:

Accountant—"I help companies/people manage their money."
Computer Programmer —"I work with technology to help businesses/my company operate more efficiently."
Costumed Team Mascot —"I'm in entertainment."
Construction worker—"I'm in the construction industry working to become a major developer."
Delivery Driver—"I'm in product distribution."
Sales—"I'm responsible for bringing new business to my company."
Fry Cook at McDonalds—"I'm a chef."
Doctor—"I'm a doctor."

Dress to Impress

A classic board game for girls called Mystery Date provides two small doors that hide pictures of the girl's fantasy dates. If the guy behind the door is dressed in a tux, she knows she is going on a dream date. If she opens the door and the guy is disheveled and dressed like a slob, she knows the date is going to be a "dud." The same guy is standing behind each door so his clothes and grooming signal whether the girl's date is going to be a dream or a dud. Think this is just a game for little girls? Don't count on it. Attractive women pay a lot of attention to the way they dress. They also pay attention to the way you dress. That's why we're going to spend some time here to get this clothes stuff straight. Don't worry, you don't need to walk around wearing a tux every day and you don't need to be a fashion slave. You should, however, pay attention to your appearance and wear at least a few quality items that fit your personal style.

WARNING FLAG

If your personal style is a Miami Vice Jacket with a thin piano-key tie it's time to find a new personal style.

There are several variables regarding how a man should dress depending on his age, budget, personal style and where he lives. However, clothing that projects a high-status image is always clean and pressed and made from fine natural fibers such as cotton, wool or silk. Women tend to prefer a man who wears clothing that accentuates the high-status "V" shape of broad shoulders and a relatively narrow waist. The right clothes and accessories can help you project an image of status that women are genetically hardwired to find attractive.

Catching a Clue about Clothes

We are going to go into some detail about how to choose, wear and care for your clothes because your clothes make such a big impression to the women you meet. When you think about it, men have it made when it comes to clothes. Imagine walking around wearing high heels, nylons and a dress. Sure, it's nice once in a while, but who wants to do it every day? And just try keeping up with the latest women's fashions. It's a full-time job that some women take very seriously. If those frilly lace undergarments didn't feel so nice against my skin, I might stop wearing women's clothing altogether. Enough about my issues. Fortunately, men's clothing is easy to figure out. Follow a few basic guidelines and you can look great with a minimum of effort.

Cut the Clutter—Do you have a dresser drawer crammed full

of socks with no match? Has your closet become a shrine for "in" fashions of the past that are now sadly "out?" Why do you keep these clothes? Do you expect an army of wayward socks to miraculously march back to their mates? Do you think skinny ties are poised to make a comeback? Do you think those tight jeans make your flabby butt look hot? While we ponder these questions, your few items of wearable clothes are crammed into a wrinkled mess hidden among a bunch of ugly rags that should have been tossed out years ago. If this is your problem, dump all your clothes into the middle of your room and don't forget your shoes. Now separate this mountain-o-clothes into three piles:

1. Looks and fits great.
2. Needs mending, alteration or cleaning.
3. "What was I thinking?"

Clothes from pile number one go back where they belong. You'll want to clean and iron these items as necessary. Put pile number two in a big plastic bag by the front door so you can have it altered or cleaned A.S.A.A. (as soon as affordable). Pile number three goes to Goodwill or gets recycled as rags for washing your car. Now, take inventory of the clothes from the first two piles so you know what you have to work with. Always remember that less is best. If a shirt looks good on you, there is nothing wrong with wearing it as often as once a week. It's better to have seven excellent shirts than 27 cheap and crappy shirts. When your clothes get room to breathe, they will have fewer wrinkles and you'll find it easier to spot what you really should be wearing.

From now on you will have to be ruthless with regard to the clothes you keep. If a favorite aunt gives you a powder blue sweater featuring a pink flower print as a birthday present, politely thank her while stealthily checking for store tags so you can exchange the item as soon as possible. You should also avoid "bargains" that aren't. Marked down clothing can be difficult to return and often the prices are lowered because other guys had the good taste to avoid the items. Only buy something on sale if it happens to be exactly what you are looking for anyway.

Buy Big Picture—The clothes you are wearing right now project a certain style. You need to ask yourself if it's a style you want to project. Mismatched clothing that fails to make a distinct statement makes you fade into the background. If your clothes are dirty, wrinkled or poorly maintained you send a message that you are lazy and really don't care about the women you meet. Why is that? Because many women are interested in fashion and you belittle that passion when you show a total disregard for what you wear. It's like when a girlfriend wears granny panties to bed every night. Doesn't she know that you have a need to see her in a G-string or a lacy garter? We all wear costumes. When you go for a job interview you wear a costume that says "successful" or "professional." When you go to a football game you wear a costume that says "sports fan." When you are in the military you wear a costume that says, well, you're in the military.

When you purchase clothing, think in terms of a costume or uniform. What is your style? Are you "Successful Steve?" "Biker Bob?" "Jack the Jock?" "Peter the Prep?" "Surfer Shawn?" "Kit the Cowboy?" "Claude the Clown?" Any of these guys, except for Claude of course, can be very attractive to large groups of women. Clowns are scary. Make sure you allow your personality and interests to dictate how you present yourself and always keep your clothes clean, pressed and well maintained. In other words, don't be a clown. Let's say you are a typical office worker but you've always been drawn to the biker lifestyle of leather and a Harley on the open road. There are many guys who wear suits during the workday and pull on leather boots and jacket at night. You might be surprised at how such a "costume" helps you unleash that biker side of your personality. Just make sure you have the Harley to back it up. You may also be surprised how women react when you present your inner style with clarity.

Shop with an Expert—A guy gets a girlfriend and suddenly he looks different. Sometimes his clothes even match. You don't need a girlfriend to start dressing better. But you should shop with a female if you want an expert's opinion on clothes that are attractive to women. She can be a friend or a stylish relative. She shouldn't be too much younger or older than you and she should be a sharp dresser herself. Most women love to shop and to show off their expertise at shopping. Just expect to wait while she does a little looking for herself. Remember that whining about the process is considered bad form. It's important to decide the purpose of the clothing before you go shopping.

If the clothes are for work, you need to follow the traditions of your industry. The clothes appropriate for work and the clothes that work best for meeting women are often very different. As I mentioned before, women tend to prefer men in clothes that fit well and accentuate the "V" shape of a thin waist and broader shoulders. They also like textures that are inviting to the touch such as leather, suede, silk, cashmere and large-pile corduroy. Why not wear clothes that make her want to reach out and touch you? Until you perfect your personal style, shop at the best stores. Nordstrom is great for a classic look. Banana Republic and Abercrombie and Fitch will have the latest styles. The Gap is fine for casual clothes. If you live in a rural area you may have to shop online. Occasionally you may find a salesperson with a good eye for helping you look your best. If you do find a winner, get the person's business card and reward him or her with your praise and repeat business.

Saving on Shoes – Shoes are important to many women (just look in their closets), so they certainly notice when a guy's shoes are less than adequate. I know some beautiful women who won't date a guy if his shoes are badly scuffed up or out of style, or if his shoes clash with his belt. Whether you wear dress shoes, tennis shoes, cowboy boots or 4-inch stiletto heels, buy quality brands that are in style and keep them clean, polished and well maintained. It comes down to a choice. Spend a few minutes polishing your shoes or spend all your time polishing Mr. Happy.

A good pair of sturdy leather shoes or boots can last up to four years with proper care. Invest $120 for a pair of quality shoes, plus $20 to have them resoled after two years and you'll spend only $35 a year on that pair of shoes. I own a pair of quality wing tips that still look great after six years of harsh treatment. On the other hand, pay $50 for a cheap pair of shoes and you may end up replacing them within six months at several times the cost of buying quality up front. Cheap leather is often harder to keep shined because you aren't dealing with the top grain of the leather. The rubber soles will quickly look shabby and your comfort may be sacrificed. And please, just say no to oversize heels, even if you are as short as Dr. Evil's "mini me." Oversize heels weigh down your look and draw too much attention to them.

Follow the Leaders—Look at the shoes that supervisors or top executives in your business are wearing. You'll notice that men in conservative businesses such as banking and accounting wear lace-up shoes with capped toes or wing tips. Men in less conservative businesses like advertising and entertainment wear more stylish shoes that slip on and they generally have thinner soles. If you work in a blue-collar job, your choice of footwear can make a big difference in protecting the health of your feet. Your supervisor will probably have strong opinions about the proper work boots to wear based on years of experience and trial and error.

Business shoes—Your shoes can help you climb to the top of the corporate ladder or grease your slide to the bottom. Buy the best you can afford and keep them in top shape. Business people and women will notice if your shoes are cheap or poorly maintained. Business shoes should be brown, burgundy or black. Black is the most formal. Cedar wood trees are a must for all your business and formal shoes. They soak up sweat and help maintain the shape of your shoes.

Formal shoes—They must be black, shiny and sleek to look good with a tux. They generally have thinner soles than conservative business shoes.

Classic casual—Topsider style boat shoes and loafers are two classic styles that work with most outfits. Don't wear socks with traditional boat shoes and always wear dark socks with loafers.

Athletic shoes—If you play a sport you will want to buy shoes designed specifically for that sport. Athletic shoes used in sports or athletic training should be replaced at least every six months of heavy use because the materials eventually break down and provide less support. Athletic shoes can be expensive so it's a good idea to wear them only when exercising or participating in your sport.

Buy socks in sets—Have you ever gotten a pair of socks as a gift and one disappeared? You might as well throw the other sock away. When you buy socks, purchase at least three identical pairs at once. If you lose a sock or wear a hole in it, you'll still have others that match.

Dress socks—They should be black, navy blue or brown to match the slacks and shoes you are wearing. Be careful about buying other colors or patterns until you are very confident in coordinating your wardrobe. No woman is going to jump your bones because of the pattern of your socks, but she may shy away if your socks clash with your outfit. Wool is the warmest and breathes a little better than synthetics, but it can be itchy. Cotton dress socks are comfortable but they tend to fade and lose their shape in the laundry, so make sure you use cool temperatures in the washer and the dryer when you launder your socks. Dress socks worn for business and special occasions must be long enough to fit over your calf so you never show skin if your pant leg hikes up. Spend a little extra to buy the Gold Toe brand (found in many department stores) and you'll find your socks hold up longer than most.

Sport socks—If you are a skier, hiker or long distance runner, you may want to experiment with some of the new synthetic socks specifically designed for your sport to cut down on blisters and breathe away sweat. Otherwise, stick with white cotton. White cotton socks are comfortable, easy to clean, tend to breathe well and won't get those tiny thread knobs that often develop on synthetic fabrics.

Panty hose—If you wear these regularly you are reading the wrong book!

Boxers and Briefs—The underwear you want cradling the family jewels is your business. Just make sure you wear briefs or a jock strap when running and exercising so your little friends aren't whipping all over the place. When you buy briefs, make sure to get them at least one size bigger than your waist size. Tight underwear is uncomfortable and can restrict your blood flow and cut down on your sperm count. No friend, tighty whities are not a reliable form of birth control, so don't even think about it! Boxers allow more air to circulate if you are trying to cut down on sweat and odor. Just make sure the crotch has a button or high opening so Willy One Eye doesn't poke his head outside the opening before it's time. Knit boxers provide the softness of briefs with the breathability of boxers. Silk boxers will make you feel naughty and she'll enjoy rubbing up against them when you get naughty.

Undershirts—V-neck undershirts were designed so a guy could take off his tie after work and not show off his undershirt. However, the V-neck may show through the fabric of some dress shirts and these days it has the rep of being an old man's undershirt. Besides, crew neck shirts tend to be more comfortable. Either way, your undershirts for work should be white and 100% cotton. For casual wear, many guys are buying designer crew neck shirts of various colors that can be worn under or without a collared shirt.

Picking Pants—Your pants should be snug enough around your waist so they don't bunch up when you tighten your belt but loose enough so you can easily pull the zipper all the way up without the pleats and pockets popping out like clown pants. Remember, clowns are scary. Often, so are pleats. Dress slacks and Khakis need to be long enough so the front crease breaks slightly about an inch above the shoe and short enough so the hem doesn't drag on the ground. Quality wool slacks are expensive but the best fabrics wear like iron, which make them worth every penny. Khakis can be 100% wool or cotton. Jeans should be 100% cotton. Don't waste your money on synthetic pants. They have gotten better in recent years but synthetics tend to block sweat, the fabric pearls and the drape of the pants start to look cheap after they've been washed a few times.

Selecting Shirts—You should be able to barely fit two fingers inside the neck when the shirt is fully buttoned up and the sleeves should be long enough so the cuffs hit the base of your hands when your arms are at your sides. Cotton breathes better than synthetics. Blended fabrics were developed to cut down on cost and provide a permanent press. The problem is that a hot iron destroys the permanent press fibers. If you like your clothes crisply pressed, as I recommend, you'll want to stick with cotton. The exception is when you are traveling. Bring a blended fabric shirt when you want to look presentable but may not get the chance to iron. Even for traveling, I suggest a blend with at least 65% cotton for comfort.

Weave—Broadcloth is a tight-weave fabric that makes a good choice for business wear because it holds a press well. Oxford is a looser weave that feels more comfortable but is also less formal. Make sure the fabric is two-ply so that it's thick enough to make sure your undershirts or chest hairs don't show through.

Colors—You can't go wrong with white. It's the preferred choice for business and formal shirts. A neutral blue is also appropriate. These colors are easy to match with suits and ties. If you venture into stripes and other colors, make sure you buy your suits, ties and shirts at the same time and enlist an expert eye to make sure they all work together.

HOT TIP

Better to Tug than Tuck—An un-tucked shirt is an obvious sign of sloppiness that can be easily avoided. The biggest problem is that most guys push their shirttails into their pants, which just bunches up the shirt below the waistline. It's better to take the time to go into a restroom so you can unbutton and unzip your pants. This allows you to reach your hands around your waist to tug the shirttail down the front, sides and back of your waist and hips. You'll be amazed at how long your shirts stay tucked when you use this technique. It also helps to keep your shirts tucked if the waist and hips of your pants fit properly.

WARNING FLAG

The guys from "Queer Eye for the Straight Guy" tend to push pink and other pastels in their makeovers of messed up men. Want some straight talk from a straight guy? Those colors are fine for casual wear to soften your look if you have dark and masculine features. If your look doesn't need softening, it's probably best to pass on the pastels.

Suiting Up

If you wear suits to work you will need at least two. Here are some key factors to consider in making your selections:

Colors—Navy blue and gray should be your first choices. The blue should be solid or feature a barely noticeable pattern. Your gray suit may be solid or feature pinstripes or a faint pattern.

Fabric—Wool will wear and fit best. If you have many suits you might consider a blend for business travel but you'll find a quality wool suit will hold up remarkably well in most conditions.

Styles—Other than for work, you will find that many fashion-conscious ladies favor the European cuts. However, stick with a standard American-style suit for work if you are in a conservative business. Two-button suits are the most traditional, but three-button suits are also appropriate for most businesses these days. On a two-button suit you only button the top button. On a three-button suit you button the middle button and occasionally the top button. The American style is best if you have a boxy or portly shape. Only try a European cut for work if you have a thin waist and work in a less conservative business. Some conservative American men distrust guys in flashy European suits and a well-tailored American suit can still look sharp and show off your physique.

Take a cue from higher-ups in your company or the company you would like to work for and always err on the side of the conservative. It's a great compliment to ask a well-dressed man where he buys his suits. If you are on the road to business success, it's worth buying your suit where you can buy quality with access to a fine tailor. If you are on a tight budget and just getting started, the private-brand Stafford Executive suits at JC Penny's is a good suit for the money. The book The Millionaire Next Door by Thomas J. Stanley, Ph.D. and William D. Danko, Ph.D. says many American millionaires buy their suits at JC Penny's. Of course, most of these millionaires own their businesses, so they presumably don't have to go out of their way to be impressive.

Test Your Tailor—If your tailor tells you he can take three inches off the waist of your suit slacks, find another suit and another tailor. Make sure to follow these steps when working with a tailor. Wear dress shoes and a dress shirt and put your wallet and keys in the pockets of the suit as you normally would so it can be altered for real life.

Trousers—The waistband should be parallel to the floor and should just touch the bottom of your navel. The pants should feel comfortable in the waist, seat and crotch, and any pleats should lie flat. Cuffs are traditional for conventional suit pants and slacks are not appropriate for most formal wear. The front crease should break slightly above the fronts of your shoes. Cuffed trousers are usually hemmed to fall straight, while hemmed trouser bottoms should slant slightly toward the back of the shoe.

A-List Accessories

Watch —Most men don't wear jewelry other than a watch, so a watch takes on special significance. People will treat you differently if you wear a Rolex on your wrist compared to one of those cheap plastic digital watches. Not everyone can afford a Rolex but a quality watch with elegant lines will get noticed. Additionally, a high-quality watch can last generations and maintain much of its value, making it worth the up-front investment.

The Truth about Ties—The modern necktie is such a powerful eye catcher that you could own one suit and dress it up with a different tie each day and few people would notice, except for the choking stench that would eventually envelope that over-worn suit and anyone who comes near it. Don't mess around with cloth, knitted or synthetic ties. Silk is generally the way to go. Don't wear clip-on ties unless you work in manufacturing where your tie could get caught in machinery, or you like being called a dweeb. The texture and color of your tie should complement your suit or blazer. A brown tweed jacket needs a tie with a more rugged texture and earthy colors. An expensive wool suit should be matched with a smooth and silky tie with rich colors. Maroon and blue are good base colors for a tie but many colors will work as long as the base color complements your suit and provides a strong contrast to the color of your shirt. The exception to this rule is the monochrome look. Buy your shirts and ties together if you are going for that look.

As a general rule, your tie will look especially sharp if accent colors match the colors of your shirt, suit or your eyes. Smaller patterns are more conservative and suggest wealth and status. Men of low status, as well as politicians and salesmen, who are trying to appeal to the common man, tend to wear ties with large and bold patterns. Generally, avoid stripes if your shirt or suit has stripes. A good rule is to wear only one striped item of clothing at one time (not counting your boxers). If you do wear two items with stripes or patterns, make sure the stripes or patterns of each item are of different proportions. You'll usually have the best luck if you buy a couple of shirts and ties when you buy a suit so you can elicit the help of an expert eye to make sure the ties complement the shirts and suit.

Time for a Good Belt—The standard width for a belt is around one inch and it should fit perfectly around your waist when the buckle is hooked on the third hole. Black is best for formal occasions, while brown and cordovan are appropriate for business and most other occasions. The buckle should be standard and simple. For business, stay away from buckles featuring designer logos. Avoid big buckles unless you are a trucker or a cowboy, and avoid suspenders unless you are a fireman on duty or a southern politician. A somewhat wider belt with a masculine steel buckle is fine for casual wear.

Wallets and Money Clips—Don't carry your wallet in a back pocket. It will ruin your pants and it makes an inviting target for pickpockets. More importantly, it forces one butt cheek higher than the other every time you sit down. This uneven posture twists your spine and eventually leads to back problems. Instead, put only your necessary credit cards, business cards and I.D. in a small credit card wallet that you wear in your front pocket. The type of wallet I'm talking about is just slightly bigger than a credit card and doesn't fold over. It should have a plastic window to display your driver's license and a few openings for credit cards and business cards.

Carry your cash in your other pocket in a sleek money clip. Have your initials engraved in the money clip for an extra touch of class. You may want to try a spring-hinged money clip because the single piece money clips eventually lose their ability to grip your cash. You'll find the small wallet and money clip setup is much more convenient. It also projects class and status for little more than you would pay for a standard wallet.

Get a lock on your laces – If you have a problem with your laces coming untied, you may be tying them incorrectly. Many guys do. Shoes are properly tied with a variation of a square knot. Some guys tie granny knots instead and don't even realize it. You can spot a granny knot because the ends of the laces lie diagonally across the shoe instead of straight across. A granny knot will also loosen itself over time. If this happens to your laces it's easy to fix.

O.K., O.K., I know we're getting all tied up with talk about laces when you're probably thinking of the frilly kind on women's underwear. But you will rarely get to that point if you have to continually pause to retie your shoes.

The key to tying a proper square knot is alternating which side wraps over the other. Since the bow part of the knot is a pattern you've been using for years, don't try to change it. Instead, pay attention to the first step of the tying process and reverse the way you wrap the laces around each other. For example, if you normally wrap your laces right-over-left during the first step, switch to left-over-right. When you finish the knot you will notice that the knot lies flat and the laces lie perpendicular across the shoe. If you really need to lock your laces, grab the ends of the laces and wrap them around each other in the same way you wrapped your laces during the first step in tying your shoes. Pull the loops tight and your laces will be locked until you untie them.

Tying a tie is pretty basic unless you don't know how. Then it can be a nightmare. Here are the steps just in case.

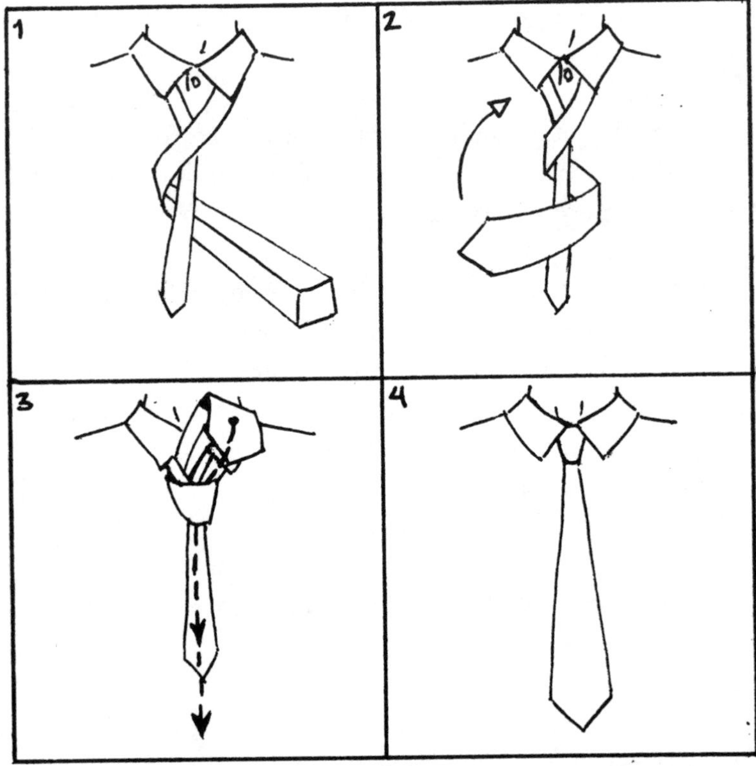

Tie One On—Four-in-hand

Start with the wide end on your right and extending 10-12" below the narrow end. Cross the wide end over the narrow and hold them together with the index finger and thumb of your right hand.

1. Wrap the wide end around the narrow end and up through the loop around your neck.
2. Feed the wide end down through the loop in front.
3. Remove finger and thumb and carefully draw the knot up to the collar while pulling the narrow end of the tie down. Grab your tie just below the knot with your middle finger and thumb and press in the center of the tie with your index finger to create a dimple just below the knot.
4. The tip of the wide end should fall between the top and bottom of your belt when you are standing up straight (which may take a couple attempts). Tying your tie, that is. Not standing up—I hope. The narrow end can be tucked through the label on the back of the wide end so that the narrow end doesn't flap around too much.

The Half-Windsor is better for wide-spread collars. The difference is that you make the loop by crossing the wide end over the narrow end and immediately up through the loop around your neck. Then proceed with steps 1-4 of the Four-in-hand knot.

Be Knot Afraid - O.K., I'm getting a little off subject here, but knowing how to tie a proper knot is a skill that truly separates the men from the morons. Plus, you can demonstrate your expertise when she asks you to tie her to the headboard. For this and other reasons there are three knots that every guy should know (see illustration on next page).

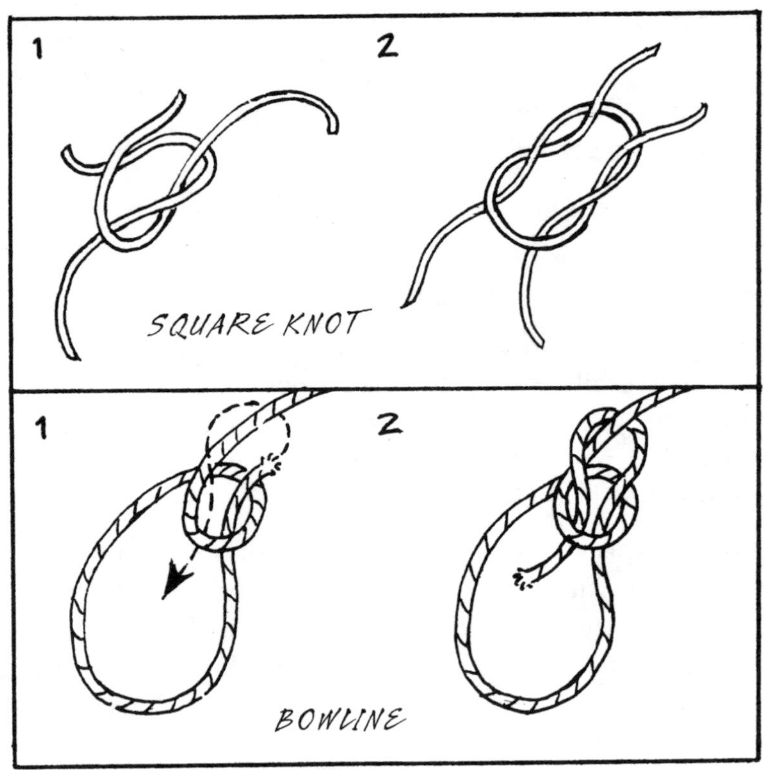

Square knot—This knot is used for tying two ends of rope together. It's a variation of the knot you use to tie your shoes if you know how to tie your shoes correctly.

1. With the rope ends facing each other, wrap one rope around the other rope (just like the first step in tying your shoes).
2. Repeat the process but this time the opposite side wraps around the other rope end, i.e., right-over-left side and then left-over-right side. If you have trouble, make sure that if you wrap one end away from you the other side should wrap away from you the second time. You will know that you have the knot right because it lies flat and looks symmetrical.

The Clove Hitch—This easy knot is used for attaching rope to a pole, a tree or a bedpost. The harder you pull on the rope, the tighter it gets.

1. Wrap the rope around the pole in a spiral with the working

end of the rope crossing over the first layer of rope.

2. As you start the second wrap, tuck the working end under the diagonal wrap of rope and pull the working end away from the original line of rope.

The Bowline—This knot separates the men from the boys. It's great for any time you need a strong loop that holds like iron. It's tightens when cinched and doesn't slip.

1. Make a simple loop in the rope and put the working end through the loop you created.
2. Wrap the working end under the stationary part of the rope and back down through the original loop. Use the illustration as a guide and remember the following mnemonic until the knot is locked in your brain: The rabbit comes out of the hole, goes around the tree and back down the hole.

Packing Your Clothes

A single guy hits the road for an overnight trip for many reasons: a work assignment, a family visit, a class reunion, an optimistic second date, etc. Whatever gets you out there, make sure you do right by your clothes. Your success may depend on it.

Avoid wrinkles—Travel light by packing items that can be mixed and matched so that your clothes are not crammed into your suitcase.

Garment bag - Hang your pants, shirts and jackets when possible. Leave items on the plastic from the dry cleaners or put sheets of gift-wrap tissue between layers so the clothes slide instead of bunching up.

Standard suitcase—Cut a piece of thick cardboard so it can lie flat inside the suitcase with at least two inches on top and bottom. Put in shoes so they line the bottom floor of the suitcase when it's standing upright. I recommend cleaning off the doggy doodoo first. Roll socks and underwear and fit them in the nooks and crannies left by your shoes. With your shirts and jackets on hangers and your pants folded over once lengthwise, lay the clothes in a neat pile on the cardboard with the hangar hooks over the top end of the cardboard. Wrap the bottom ends of your clothes around the other end of the cardboard and put the clothes and cardboard in the suitcase so that the fold is at the top and the top and bottoms of your clothes hang down when the suitcase is carried upright. You will still get a few wrinkles. You can use a wrinkle releasing spray or just use the old trick of hanging the wrinkled clothes in the bathroom with the shower on hot and the door closed to fill the room with steam.

Packing Checklist:

(None of these items will stop wrinkles, but you'll miss them if you forget them.)

- ❑ Razor and shaving cream (not for carry-on commercial aircraft) or electric razor
- ❑ Toothpaste
- ❑ Toothbrush
- ❑ Nail clippers (not for carry-on commercial aircraft)
- ❑ Travel alarm clock
- ❑ Pocketknife (not for carry-on commercial aircraft)
- ❑ Deodorant
- ❑ Cologne or aftershave
- ❑ Shampoo
- ❑ Pain reliever
- ❑ Water

With heightened airport security and the possibility your bags will be checked, you might want to leave your collection of Young Teens In Tight Jeans magazines at home.

The Dirt on Cleaning and Maintenance—How many clothes have you ruined in the wash? Here are the top ten ways to make sure it doesn't happen again.

1. Never fill the washer or dryer more than two-thirds full. Overfilled washers won't get clothes as clean as possible and an overfilled dryer will damage your clothes from too much time tumbling in the hot air.

2. Separate clothes into white, light and dark. It's a good idea to wash bath towels separately from your other clothes if you have a lot of towels to wash.
3. Wash a new article of clothing separately if the color is red or another bright color.
4. Avoid hot water unless the fabrics are sturdy and white or you are trying to shrink an item of cotton clothing.
5. Put the soap in first as the tank starts to fill. Then add clothes.
6. Use bleach sparingly; use liquid bleach only on whites and never pour bleach directly onto clothes.
7. Take the clothes from the washer soon after the spin cycle is done and take them out of the dryer before they are overly dry.
8. Don't dry clothes with high heat unless you are trying to shrink them.
9. Permanent press clothes need a cool-down stage at the end of the drying process to minimize wrinkles.
10. Stop the dryer as soon as the clothes are just barely dry and fold them immediately. If you forget, you can put a wet towel with the clothes in the dryer and let them tumble together for a few minutes to minimize wrinkles.

Stains—Most stains will come out if you blot them right away with water and liquid dishwashing detergent. It helps to put a towel under the stain when you blot it clean. A product called K2r works pretty well on dry-cleanable and man-made fabrics. First you spray on the absorbent powder and then you brush away the powder (and hopefully the spot with it). For mixed drinks, fruit drinks, mustard, ketchup, coffee and tea, dab them with a 5-to-1 water and vinegar solution before rinsing with water. For milk, blood and other animal stains, rub them with a 2-to-1 water and ammonia solution before rinsing with water. If former President Clinton had used this stain-fighting technique, we might never have learned about Monica's blue dress. Now you know better than a president! For oil, grease and ink stains, use a solvent-based stain remover such as Spray and Wash.

Ironing

Shirts—Take them straight from the wash and hang them on wood or plastic hangers before the shirts are completely dry. Use a little spray starch and iron them on the wide end of the ironing board. Start with the collar, then each side of the back, then the sleeves and shoulder area. Finally, carefully iron the front panels of the shirt.

Pants—Turn them inside out and iron everything but the crease on the pants legs. Rub a bar of soap along the inside crease to make the crease sharper when it's ironed. Turn the pants back out and turn the iron down about halfway to iron just the crease and other wrinkles you may have missed. You want to avoid high heat because it can cause shiny spots. Wool pants should almost always be pressed by professional dry cleaners.

Dry Cleaners

The chemicals and heat used by many dry cleaners eventually destroy the fabric of dry-cleaned clothes. However, some clothes must be dry-cleaned and the look and convenience of dry-cleaning make it worthwhile for many guys.

Wool suits, slacks and blazers and silk shirts: Dry clean only and only dry clean when necessary. Your wool and silk clothes will last a lot longer if you only dry clean them when they get a stain or start to stink.

Dress shirts: Experiment with how many shirts you can iron in an hour and find out how much it would cost to have that many shirts professionally cleaned and pressed. If it takes you an hour to iron four shirts and costs you $8 to have that many shirts cleaned and pressed, it's probably worthwhile to have your shirts professionally cleaned (as long as you make at least $8 an hour). Just make sure you check for broken buttons, remaining stains and misplaced creases before you take them from the dry cleaners. Don't be afraid to ask them to fix errors.

Stains: Tell the cleaners about any stains you want removed. They will mark the stains and work to remove them. Otherwise, the stains will be much harder to remove after the clothes have been cleaned.

Ties: They rarely survive dry cleaning and rarely look the same afterward. Ask around in your area for a drycleaner that specializes in cleaning ties. I have rarely been happy with the results. Unfortunately, if you can't get the stain out yourself, it's probably time to kiss the tie goodbye.

Camouflage Your Flaws

Most of us have something about our physical appearance that we would like to change. Wouldn't it be great if you could look thinner, heavier or even taller just by wearing the right clothes? You can! Let's talk some basic do's and don'ts:

Look Thinner

Do—Find a good tailor and buy the suits he recommends. A good tailor can work miracles.

Do—Wear jackets with padded shoulders so your upper body looks bigger than your waist.

Do—Choose long and pointed collars to make your face and jaw look longer.

Don't—Wear thick or fuzzy fabrics or several layers because they add girth.

Don't—Wear tight fitting clothes if you are pudgy because they will show fat bulges. Fitted clothes are great if your body is stocky but toned.

Don't—Wear horizontal lines or patterns because they draw the eye out.

Don't—Keep eating all those fatty foods and refined carbohydrates. There is only so much that clothes can camouflage.

Look Heavier

Do—Wear shirts and pants that contrast in color to break up the visual line made by your body.

Do—Wear cuffed and (consider) pleated pants to draw people's attention outward.

Do—Wear tall collars and turtlenecks to hide a long neck. Measure the height of a collar from the back.

Do—Wear spread collars to broaden your face.

Do—Wear rough and fuzzy fabrics, sweaters and layers.

Don't—Wear extremely loose fitting clothes because they can make you look like a walking hanger.

Don't—Wear vertical stripes and patterns.

Look Taller

Do—Wear pants, belt and shirt of the same or similar color so your legs and torso form a continuous line to the eye.

Do—Wear fitted jackets and coats or tighten the belt of your overcoat to make a narrower silhouette.

Don't —Wear a sport jacket of a color that contrasts dramatically with your slacks because that causes a visual break that cuts your body into two short segments.

Don't—Wear pleated trousers, cuffed trousers, too much padding in the shoulders, wide lapels, wide ties or bow ties. All these clothing features draw attention out instead of up.

Don't—Wear excessively large heels because their bulky appearance draws too much attention down to your feet and weighs down your look.

Don't—Date a woman significantly taller than yourself. But if you do, make sure you take her slow dancing.

Whew, you made it through the dress-up section! If you follow the advice in this chapter, you will take a huge step into the world of the Modern Alpha Male. Now relax, it's Dress Down Day from now on.

Chapter 4

WE WERE MADE FOR EACH OTHER

PHYSICAL SUPERIORITY—BUILD A BETTER BODY

Unfortunately, the right clothes can only do so much to maximize a guy's perceived height. When women are surveyed, they consistently show a preference for men of average or above average height. Five feet and eleven inches tall is most often given as the ideal height for a marriage partner. Tall men tend to hold higher status in nearly all cultures. In the West, tall men make more money and advance in their professions faster. So does that mean if you're 5'7" you are doomed to a lonely life of height-imposed celibacy? Hardly! Tom Cruise at 5'7" could rightfully challenge the notion that women prefer taller men. He is a perfect example of how a man's positive qualities can easily overcome those perceived as lacking. Cruise has so much wealth, status and ambition that women are happy to overlook the fact that he's somewhat vertically challenged. His extreme athleticism and fitness help him compensate for a little lack of height. Cruise is living proof that shorter guys can get all the beautiful skirt they want. But just in case you aren't a rich and famous movie star, here are a couple of steps you can use in conjunction with wearing the proper clothes to help you maximize your perceived height.

It is better to have loved a small man than never to have loved a tall.

- Mary Jo Crowley

Add an Inch Where It Counts—Let's talk basics here:

1. Posture—If your head protrudes forward like a turtle and your body is perpetually slouching, you create the impression of being at least one inch shorter than your actual height. O.K., on this point your mom's nagging was valid. Put your back against the wall. If you have bad posture you will only touch the wall with your butt and your upper back. Take a moment for some posture boot camp. Atten…tion! Pull that stomach in, chest up and out and shoulders and head back. This straightens your spinal column and increases your height. It helps to think of a straight line passing through the top of your head and spine. Poor posture can be a hard habit to break. You'll need to be your own drill instructor and pay attention to your posture for at least three weeks to make the new taller posture automatic.

2. Orthotic and sport cushion insoles—Wearing quality insoles in your shoes increases your height in two ways. First, there is the physical thickness of the insole. Second, a proper insole will help you stand and walk with better posture by aligning your body forward. Most insoles available at the grocery store are relatively flimsy and fail to provide the support of the expensive, semi-custom versions you can buy at specialty shoe stores. Sport cushion insoles are less expensive

and can be found in most sporting goods stores. Sport insoles don't provide the support or posture benefits of a good orthotic insole, but they do add some spring and added comfort to your shoes, as well as about half an inch to your height. You'll want to bring the inserts or insoles with you when you purchase shoes because it may be necessary to purchase shoes slightly larger than you normally would. You can always tell the shoe salesman that they help your feet. It's the truth.

Making a Mountain Out of a Molehill

Another area where an inch really counts is that nether region between a guy's legs. You've probably heard that the average size penis is about six inches long and that most women don't care much about size as long as it's near that average…blah, blah, blah. Regardless of what some women might say, we men know that bigger is better and we want our guy to be one of those bigger ones. Because of this demand, surgical and non-surgical techniques that promise to lengthen and widen the penis are marketed extensively and often unethically. Many of these techniques have serious potential side effects and most simply don't work. The good news is that three techniques do work and I'm hanging down to my knees. I wish. The truth is there are three techniques that will make Mr. Happy at least appear to be somewhat larger. Before we cover these effective techniques, here is a brief summary of the most common surgical and non-surgical techniques for penis enlargement currently on the market:

Surgical procedures—Penile widening and lengthening procedures have been shown to work for many patients but they can have serious side effects. The widening procedure involves using fat from another part of your body or specially treated donor flesh and inserting it under the skin of the penis. Potential complications include the following: absorption of the fat, failure of the graft to take, scarring, fibrosis of a superficial vein, shortening of the penis, infection, bleeding, bruising, decrease in penile sensation, temporary swelling of the penis, a collection of serum under the skin, loss of penile skin and erectile dysfunction. Penile lengthening involves the release of the suspensory ligament that attaches the two erectile bodies of the penis to the pubic bone. The suspensory ligament makes the penis arch under the pubic bone. Release of this ligament allows the penis to protrude further outward to give more length. Weights are sometimes applied to the penis after the surgery for a few months to maximize the amount that the penis protrudes from the body. Average length gain is about one inch. The risks of penile lengthening surgery include: a reduction of the erect upward angle of the penis, a scar at the site of the incision, fibrosis of a superficial vein, shortening of the penis, skin incision separation, bruising, bleeding, infection, temporary swelling of the penis, a collection of serum under the skin, reduction in penile sensation, erectile dysfunction. Have I scared you yet? Bottom line is that the American Urological Association, Inc.® (AUA) considers subcutaneous fat injection for increasing penile girth, and the division of the suspensory ligament of the penis for increasing penile length to be "procedures which have not been shown to be safe or efficacious." There are also several non-surgical techniques of penile lengthening on the market. Unfortunately, none have been proven to work in medical studies and some have serious potential side effects.

Penis pumps—A man who suffers from weak erections or impotence due to diabetes or circulatory disorders can use a penis pump to obtain a full erection. Once an erection is achieved, the penis is removed from the cylinder and the blood is prevented from escaping by placing a constriction band around the base of the penis. A temporary increase in size is also possible with a penis pump. However, there are no credible studies to confirm claims of any long-term benefits. Additionally, I've read horror stories that men who pump too frequently for extended periods of time, or apply too much vacuum pressure, run the risk of rupturing capillaries and blood vessels. This can result in large bruises and water blisters appearing on the penile shaft or red spots developing on the head of the penis. I'm getting grossed out just writing about this.

Weights and other stretching devices—Hanging weights from the penis and other stretching techniques have been tried for thousands of years. In theory, these methods should work to some degree because human flesh and ligaments have the ability to stretch somewhat over time. Additionally, weights are often used after penis lengthening surgeries to maximize gains. However, flesh and ligaments are also very elastic so it would take almost constant stretching to maintain any gains. Additionally, depending upon the stretching device being used, blood circulation may be decreased or cut off, which could, in turn, cause necrosis (death) of the tissue. There are simply no reputable medical studies to measure the long-term effectiveness or side effects of stretching techniques on the penis. You are taking a big risk with a very important part of your body if you try one of these techniques.

Enlargement pills—If any pill worked to safely and permanently enlarge the penis, you wouldn't just read about it in spam emails. You would hear about it on every newscast and read about it in every newspaper. Viagra would be an afterthought compared to the popularity of such a pill. It would be quite simple to scientifically prove the effectiveness of such a pill, and the inventor of the enlargement pill would be the richest guy on the planet. If you check the ingredients of these so-called enlargement pills, you will notice that they contain many of the same active ingredients contained in herbal sexual enhancement pills. Some of these pills work to help guys get stronger erections more often. But you don't need to pay the outrageous prices of enlargement pills when you can get the same results with a good herbal sexual enhancement pill.

Penis Enlargement that Works

Infrapubic fat reduction—If a guy is overweight with a protruding gut, it's very likely he has an extra layer of fat over the pubic bone around the base of the penis. This infrapubic fat pad may hide as much as one inch of the length of the penis in some overweight men. Losing a substantial amount of fat from that area will, in many cases, expose that extra length of penis. The fat can be removed using lyposuction or, preferably, through good diet and exercise. Resulting health benefits from losing the fat should also improve your erections, sex drive and sexual stamina. Not to mention your attractiveness to the ladies. Later in this chapter we will discuss a comprehensive system to help you quickly lose fat from your midsection.

Trimming pubic hair —A thick mat of pubic hair can hide a portion of the base of the penis. Trimming back the pubic hair will expose more of the shaft and enhance the apparent length of the penis. This process also helps minimize body odor in that region because pubic hair can become a breeding ground for odor-causing bacteria. Women will appreciate that you are well groomed where it really counts.

Herbal sexual enhancement pills—As I mentioned before, no pill has been proven to permanently increase the size of the penis. However, there are herbal pills that work to encourage increased blood flow to the penis while you are taking the pills. These pills tend to make the penis more swollen when flaccid and also maximize the size and firmness of an erection. Every guy has experienced times when his flaccid penis is somewhat engorged with blood and appears larger than usual and there are also times when an erection stands especially tall and firm. The best herbal enhancement pills make those experiences more of the norm as long as a guy keeps taking the pills. Now, I'm not a doctor and I don't know about any health issues you may be dealing with, so I can't say herbal sexual enhancement pills will be safe or effective for you. All I can say is that I tried a couple of brands as research for this book (sounded like a good excuse to me) and it was like high school all over again.

All right, time to move from the little head to the big head. Don't worry, we won't try to make your noggin look bigger, just better.

The Right Cut

A new hairstyle is one of the fastest and easiest ways to dramatically change your appearance. When looking for a stylist or barber, don't just pop into a salon and hope for the best. Ask for recommendations from guys you know who actually have good haircuts. The style and length of your hair is a matter of personal preference. But the wrong cut can limit your opportunities in the job market as well as the meat market. Some young women with rebellious tendencies are attracted to long locks. Most women will be happy if you actually have hair and keep it clean and well groomed. If your cut is stylish and flatters your face, all the better.

Narrow face—Grow your hair a little fuller on the sides to give thickness to your face. Don't cut it too short on top or it will look out of proportion with your face. If you part your hair, the part should be located closer to the center of your head to draw attention away from the sides of your face. Let the hair drape down in front to cover a high forehead. The sideburns should be cut at or above the cheekbone to widen your face. Hair that is a little longer and fuller behind the ears can help to camouflage a long, thin neck. Don't overdo it, though. I wouldn't recommend that any guy get a mullet.

Round face—Hair should be fuller to create a frame around a large, round face. Part hair over to the side with sideburns cut lower than the cheekbone. Comb hair across the top of the forehead to complete the frame.

Pear-shaped face—Wide jowls make the face narrow at the top and wide at the bottom. Keep your hair relatively thick at the crown, and temples short, so that it ends above the jawline and provides balance to the lower part of your face.

Prominent nose—Balance a prominent nose by bringing the hair forward at the forehead and back at the sides.

Thinning hair—A slight receding hairline can be covered with a part toward the center of the head or no part at all and the front hair combed over the receding temples. If your hair starts to thin or recede significantly, cut all the hair short so that the thinning areas won't stand out.

Beards and mustaches—Facial hair will generally make you look older. The right beard can disguise a weak or overly large chin. It will also cover damaged skin. A mustache can conceal a large or thin upper lip. On the downside, facial hair must be carefully groomed or you'll look scraggly and it turns some women off—especially when food gets stuck in it for days at a time.

Six-pack Abs in 6 to 12 Weeks

I'm not a fitness expert but I've trained with world-class body builders and I've had six-pack abs myself. In full disclosure, I'm barely sporting a four-pack these days. No doubt caused by drinking too many six packs. Regardless, I can certainly give you a few useful pointers if you are willing to put in the work. Any guy in decent physical shape has the foundation of a six-pack. Unfortunately, it's hidden under a thick layer of fat. Strong abdominal muscles are important for your athletic performance and will help you avoid back problems. But the key to six-pack abs is removing the layer of fat around your midsection. The CBS show "Survivor" showed us how abdominal muscles start to pop once body fat is removed. In fact, the best way to develop an attractive midsection is to develop your whole body because increased muscle mass speeds your metabolism and helps your body to more quickly burn fat.

The most efficient way that I've found for the average guy to get ripped abs incorporates weight training, sprinting, good nutrition and nutritional supplements. You could write entire books on this subject and many people have. Unfortunately, much of the workout advice from professional body builders isn't completely applicable to the average guy because they often take steroids to compete at that level. People on steroids can train much longer than natural bodybuilders. If you are not on the "juice" (which is a good thing) you need to be much more careful about over stressing your nervous system and losing muscle through over-training. A couple of bodybuilders who also happen to be brothers have written excellent books on how to get results with natural bodybuilding. Bill Phillips has a best-selling book called Body for Life and his brother Shawn wrote a great book called AbSolution. My suggestions are generally consistent with the advice in both of the books listed above, but those guys provide much more information on the specific techniques as well as the important psychological element involved in building a better body.

My goal in this book is to hit on some of the key strategies that have really worked for me to get you started on the right path.

Supercharge with Supplements

The supplement business rakes in billions of dollars a year and throws out a lot of claims to keep the money flowing in. Don't let the hype and the confusing claims empty your pocketbook. New "miracle" supplements come out every day, but I prefer to wait until they are backed up by scientific studies. Numerous scientific and university studies have proven the effectiveness of three nutritional supplements: protein powder, creatine and conjugated linoleic acid (CLA). You can find these items in almost any health food or supplement store. With these supplements and a good multivitamin plus a well-balanced diet, you should be able to get all the nutritional fuel you need to get great results.

Protein powder comes in many forms. A quality whey protein will work fine for most guys. You can mix it with water or milk and add a little fruit for taste to make a healthy smoothie as a between-meal snack. Creatine is sold just about everywhere these days. You need to "load" it for the first week, which means taking a large amount as described on the packaging. You want to drink lots of water because the creatine can make you dehydrated. You can also boost results by taking your Creatine with grape juice or using a brand of Creatine that includes insulin-releasing carbohydrates. CLA is a compound of fat that has been clinically proven to burn fat while maintaining lean muscle. You can find CLA in any good health food or supplement store and it's relatively cheap. All you do is take three to four capsules before meals and watch the fat slowly melt away. While we're on the subject of losing fat, I've found that drinking a cup of green tea in the morning is a healthy way to keep your metabolism revving. Green tea is loaded with healthy antioxidants and it contains less caffeine than coffee.

Six steps to six-pack abs:

1. Weight Training—Before eating in the morning, drink a large glass of water and train intensely with weights for no more than one hour, three times a week.

How: The first week, train your upper body Monday and Friday and legs on Wednesday. The second week, switch to legs on Monday and Friday and train your upper body on Wednesday. Start with larger muscles such as your chest, back or thighs. Do 12 reps the first set as a warm-up and then lift 8 to 10 reps each set for 3 more sets. Allow only 30 seconds to one minute between sets and increase the weight and intensity with each set of a given body part. The key is intensity. Constantly strive to increase the weight you lift while maintaining good form. The tried and true exercises work great so there is little reason to get fancy for the first couple of months. After that, you may see your gains level off and that's a great time to mix up your routine with another set of exercises. You can learn proper technique for the following exercises in any good weightlifting book.

Upper body
Chest—bench press and flyes
Shoulders—military press and side raises
Back—wide-grip pull downs and dumbbell rows
Triceps —dumbbell extensions and bench dips
Biceps—dumbbell and preacher curls

Lower body
Quadriceps —squats or leg presses
Hamstrings—lunges and leg curls
Calves—seated and standing calf raises

Why: Training before breakfast causes your body to burn fat for fuel instead of your breakfast. A short and intense workout shocks the muscles without overstressing your nervous system. Giving each muscle group proper rest between workouts allows you to avoid the common problem of diminished results caused by over-training. Weight training breaks down the muscle. The muscle rebuilds during the rest period after a workout.

2. Sprints

What: Run sprints for up to 20 minutes three times a week before breakfast.

How: Alternate a minute of sprinting for each minute of jogging Tuesday, Thursday and Saturday mornings. Start with 10 minutes and work up to 20 minutes of sprints.

Why: Look at a sprinter's body compared to a long-distance runner's body and you'll see why I recommend sprinting. You'll notice that the sprinter is muscular and cut while the marathon runner is just plain skinny. Sprinting shoots your metabolism through the roof, pumps your body with growth hormones and burns fat long after you've stopped sprinting. Running for long periods of time burns muscle as well as fat.

3. Abdominal Exercises

What: Exercise abdominal muscles right after your morning sprints, and exercise abs no more than three times a week. The abdominal workout should incorporate three supersets with each one featuring three different exercises to effectively target the upper abs, lower abs and obliques in every abdominal workout.

How: Start with the old-fashioned crunch: raise your shoulders while your lower back and feet are kept flat on the floor. Lie on your back with knees bent and together, feet flat on the floor about a foot from your butt and hands beside your head (don't lock your hands behind your head). It's just like you want your women without the knees together business. Focus on contracting the abdominal muscles before you begin. Push your lower back into the mat and slowly roll your shoulders up while keeping your neck straight. Flex your abs tightly and raise your torso until your upper back starts to lift off the floor. Hold the position for a two-count before slowly lowering your back and shoulders back down to the mat. Do 12 reps breathing out during the contraction and breathing in as you lower your torso. A great variation of the floor crunch is to use a Swiss Ball under your back. You'll need to keep your feet about shoulder-width apart for balance. The Swiss Ball allows for a greater range of motion, and the effort to balance on the ball improves the exercise.

Without resting, switch immediately to a side crunch. Side crunches are similar to regular crunches with your knees bent and hands beside your head except with side crunches your torso is twisted to allow one of your legs to lie flat on the floor with the other leg lying on top. With your upper body facing upward, contract your abdominal muscles and lift your upper body off the floor as you exhale. Hold the contraction for a two-count before starting your exhale and slowly lowering yourself back to the starting position. Do a set 12 on each side and always remember to breathe during each rep.

Without resting, position yourself for a reverse crunch to target the lower abs. The position is very similar to a regular crunch except your feet start about six inches off the floor. Contract your abdominal muscles while slowly curling your lower body up toward your shoulders. Exhale as you roll your hips off the mat. When your hips and lower back are slightly off the floor, hold the contraction for a two-count and slowly lower your hips to the starting position. A set of 12 slow reps with proper form will really rock your lower abs. Rest your abs for 60 seconds between supersets. Stretch your abs as you rest by lying on your back with your arms stretched straight over your head. You may want to start doing just two abdominal supersets for the first week. Proper form is more important than the number of repetitions. Work up to three supersets by the second week. You can work in other abdominal exercises to your program if these get boring. Just make sure that you target all three regions of the abdominals with a three-exercise superset.

Why: It's important to do exercises that work the three major regions of the abdominal muscles. Doing your abdominal workout on the same days as your sprinting workout allows you to focus on your abs. Your abdominal muscles develop in the same way as your other muscles so high intensity and good form is much more effective than doing hundreds of repetitions. You know, kind of like sex. O.K., back to the abs. You want to give your abdominal muscles time to rest and repair between workouts. Many people are building great endurance with their frequent high-rep workouts, but they aren't building great-looking abs.

HOT TIP

The Ab Vacuum is a highly effective and relatively unknown abdominal exercise practiced by some of the top bodybuilders in the world. Three-time Mr. Universe Frank Zane taught me this technique several years ago when I was lucky enough to train with him. If you want more details, I recommend you read Frank's book *Fabulously Fit Forever.* One reason I love the ab vacuum is that it can be done virtually anywhere, anytime and it exercises the often forgotten transverse abdominis muscle (inner abs). To learn this exercise, lie on your back with your knees bent and feet flat on the mat. Rest your head on the mat with your arms at your sides. Exhale all the air out of your lungs and hold your exhale. Now pull your belly in and up as if you are trying to touch your belly to your spine. Hold your belly in for a long two-count before allowing yourself to inhale. I do one set of 12 reps of the Ab Vacuum to finish off my abdominal workout. Once you get the hang of the Ab Vacuum, you can do a set while driving in your car or standing in line for a lap dance.

4. Eat Many Mini-meals

What: Eat five to six balanced, low-fat meals six days a week and make sure each meal contains lean protein such as egg whites, skinless chicken breast or turkey breast, fish, top sirloin steak or protein powder.

How: The portions of each meal should be small and you want to make sure you include fruit with at least one meal and plenty of green vegetables with at least two of those daily meals. Fitness expert Bill Phillips recommends portions about the size of your palm for meat (although I hate to use palm and meat in the same sentence, that guideline has always worked for me). Premixed nutrition drinks such as Myoplex or Met-Rx provide plenty of protein and make good meal replacements for one or two of your daily meals. A great time for a protein shake is right after your workout because the protein will digest quicker so your body can benefit sooner. The seventh day you can splurge and eat whatever you want (I still limit cake and cookies).

Why: When you eat only two or three meals a day your body starts to go into hunger mode between meals. This lowers your metabolism and causes your body to store fat. Long breaks between meals also tend to cause cravings that can prompt you to overeat. When you eat a small balanced meal with lean protein every few hours, it regulates your insulin levels and tells your body that there is no reason to store fat. Splurging one day a week may help convince your body that it's not starving and helps you resist cheating the rest of the week.

5. Drink Plenty of Water

What: Drink six to eight glasses of water each day.

How: Carry a large water bottle with you and drink from it throughout the day. You may also consider heating water in your coffee cup and sipping on the hot water instead of your morning cup of coffee.

Why: Your body will operate much better if it's properly hydrated. Many of the beverages we drink bring unpleasant consequences. Coffee and alcohol cause dehydration, sugared sodas and fruit drinks spike insulin levels and cause our bodies to store fat.

6. Rest

What: Maximize muscle-building by getting plenty of rest and sleep.

How: It's a good idea to get eight to nine hours of sleep when you are in training.

Why: This will provide your nervous system with plenty of rest and allow your body to repair and rebuild your muscles.

The workouts in this program take less than an hour a day if you plan well. The key is to consistently apply all six steps. It's a commitment, but you'll find the results are well worth it. There is nothing better than watching a women's mouth drop when you take your shirt off.

Banish Bad Breath and Body Odor

The Mouth that Roared: She is a modern day princess and her eyes say you might be her knight in shining armor. You charge over and gallantly start a conversation. She falls over dead. Why does this keep happening? Maybe it's your breath. One whiff and it's goodbye knight in shining armor, hello fire-breathing dragon. And damsels aren't the only ones in distress. Everyone suffers. Fear not. You can slay that dragon and also make your teeth shine brighter than any knight's armor.

Where the Dragon Lurks: Like a dark moist cave, your mouth makes a perfect lair for anaerobic sulfur-causing bacteria. These bacteria live on the tongue, roof of your mouth, throat, tonsils (if present) and between teeth. Stress, gum disease and sinus infections can make matters worse and certain foods contribute to the problem. However, fumes from your stomach are only a minor source of dragon breath for most people. Here are some of the biggies:

Dairy foods—Many people lack an enzyme called lactose that is necessary to break down proteins found in milk, cheese and ice cream. The bad breath bacteria love to feed on the dairy proteins and that causes bad breath.

Garlic and onions—These foods are notorious for bad breath because they contain sulfur compounds that can really stink up your breath.

Coffee—Bacteria reproduces rapidly in the acidic environment caused by coffee, which is why coffee breath can hit almost instantly.

Sugar and foods made with processed sugar—Bacteria thrive in a sugary environment, which is why the use of mints and candies can actually make your breath worse.

Alcohol—Whether in mixed drinks, wine, beer or even mouthwash, alcohol dries the mouth rapidly, which causes bad breath. This is one reason you should stay away from mouthwashes containing alcohol. Additionally, drink plenty of water when you are having drinks that contain alcohol.

Choose Your Weapons

A plastic tongue scraper can help you remove odor-causing bacteria prior to brushing. A soft-bristled toothbrush or the front edge of a plastic spoon will also work in a pinch.

When you are brushing your teeth and the inside of your mouth, always use a soft-bristled toothbrush. The hard-bristled brushes work great for cleaning the grout between floor tiles but they are far too rough on teeth and gums.

Use floss that is both waxed and flavored. The wax allows the floss to slip easily between your teeth. The flavoring helps your mouth smell and taste as fresh as possible.

Use a mouthwash that doesn't contain alcohol because the alcohol can dry out the inside of your mouth and make halitosis worse.

Sonic toothbrushes such as Sonic Air work to disrupt smelly plaque even below the gum line—if you can afford to spend $80 plus on a toothbrush.

Attack!

After breakfast and before bed:

Put some toothpaste on a plastic tongue scraper and lightly scrape the top surface of your tongue several times. Rinse with water.

Put more toothpaste on your toothbrush and brush the roof of your mouth, inside your cheeks and your tongue, reaching as far back as possible without making yourself gag. Now you know how women feel.

Brush teeth for at least 60 seconds, directing the bristles away from the gum line at a 45-degree angle to remove as much food and plaque as possible.

Hold floss between your hands so that it's fairly loose as you pull it between the teeth and the gum line so that it wraps around the tooth. Pull tighter as you slide the floss out to scrape away the food and plaque.

Rinse well and gargle with a mouthwash that does not contain alcohol for at least 60 seconds.

HOT TIP

All of these techniques will be more effective if you use a product such as TheraBreath that contains Chlorine Dioxide.

During the Day: Brush your teeth after mid-day meals whenever possible and drink plenty of fluids (especially water). Occasionally snack on fruits and raw vegetables such as oranges, apples, peaches, carrots and celery. You'll also want to avoid dairy products, spicy and pungent foods and coffee.

If these techniques and products don't work for you, you probably have a medical problem such as a sinus infection or trouble with your digestive system. See your doctor or a specialist.

Follow all of these eating and hygiene suggestions consistently and you'll rarely have problems with your breath. You could also end up pushing your mouth into a flavor-deprived coma. Burgers without onions? Italian food without garlic? You might as well pluck out your taste buds, right? And who wants to carry around a toothbrush? I can almost hear her saying, "Is that a toothbrush in your pocket or are you just happy to see me?" No, you need some backup weapons in your arsenal for the fight against bad breath.

You can temporarily mask some minor breath odors by sucking on a sugar-free breath mint. Remember to avoid products with sugar because that will actually assist the odor causing bacteria to thrive in your mouth.

Most bars and nightclubs have a ready supply of lemon or lime wedges for mixed drinks. Chew on a citrus wedge, especially the rind, and rinse your mouth with water. A good rinsing is important because otherwise the citric acid in the rind can harm the enamel of your teeth.

Drink plenty of water. A dry mouth exaggerates breath problems.

If you are at a restaurant that still serves parsley with your meal, you can try the old trick of chewing on a piece of the parsley. Just check to make sure you don't leave any parsley bits stuck between your teeth.

Sugarless gum and sprays are two of the best products for fighting bad breath when you are on the go. Look for products that contain Chlorine Dioxide, which is one of the most effective ingredients for fighting Dragon Breath.

Care for Skin and Hair

Pepe Le Pew could be you: If you've ever watched classic cartoons, you've probably stumbled across a character named Pepe Le Pew. He's a little skunk who hops his way through life thinking he is a great Casanova. Pepe has all the suave moves but fails to notice that everyone around him is trying to escape his odiferous embrace. Unfortunately, the truth stinks for many guys. A person's nose tends to filter out the smell of his own body odor and a woman's nose tends to be more sensitive than a man's. Want to risk it? Didn't think so.

Shopping for Soap: There's nothing like stepping into a warm shower and reaching into a puddle of clumpy soap ooze. Liquid soap or a bath gel will keep your soap dish free from soap scum. Isn't your bathroom scummy enough already? Liquid soaps are an especially good idea if you share a bathroom with a roommate. Think of the last place your roommate may have rubbed the soap and the first place you use it. Enough said?

For extra odor protection, experiment with deodorant soaps containing antiseptic or antibacterial agents. These soaps require consistent use for a few days before reaching their odor fighting potential, so give them time to work. Stay away from "bargain" soaps and strongly scented soaps. Some brands may cause an allergic reaction on your skin or irritate your sinuses.

Better Bathing

Bathing is like being an auto mechanic. You spend most of your time working in the pits.

Lather some soap in your hands and give your whole body a quick once-over. Then go back to gently scrub your armpits, crotch and feet. The scrubbing helps remove antiperspirant residue, old skin and odor-causing bacteria. A shower sponge or washcloth adds friction to clean more thoroughly, but you need to make sure these items are well rung out and hung up to dry so they don't become a ripe environment for bacteria and mildew.

Rinse your skin well and before you grab a towel, skim off the excess water with your hands using a quick downward motion along your torso, arms and legs. Competitive swimmers use this trick to make sure their towels don't get over saturated before they fully dry off. When you do grab for a towel, make sure it's clean and smells fresh. Bath towels and washcloths should be laundered after no more than three uses and they need to be hung spread out so they dry quickly. There is little sense in taking a shower just to wipe a dirty towel loaded with the smell of mildew all over your body.

If You Smell Like a Bear, Trim that Hair

Your body hair may be a source of manly pride, but it can also create a bear of an odor problem. Hair under your arms and around your crotch creates a cozy home for odor-causing bacteria. Shave or trim back those areas about twice a month and you will dramatically cut down on your body odor. This may seem weird at first, but lots of guys do it because it really makes a difference.

Deodorant Don'ts

Don't feel that you have to stick with that musk or herb-scented product because it smells "manly." Do you really want to smell like a sweaty herb? Experiment with "clean," "fresh," and "regular" scented deodorants until you find one that works for you.

Don't wear antiperspirant unless you have reason to be concerned about excessive sweat. The aluminum chlorhydrate and other chemicals in antiperspirants work by clogging your pores. Allow your body to sweat once in a while by using a deodorant without antiperspirant, especially if you are just hanging with the guys and you'll get a chance to shower afterward.

HOT TIP

If you have a problem with yellow stains developing in the armpits of your shirts, try Weleda deodorant found in many health food stores.

Pat on Some Powder

Millions of babies' butts can't be wrong. Powder works great at absorbing moisture and odor for guys with sweat problems. Some guys use it as a cheap and effective supplement to antiperspirant for body parts other than the armpits. Just don't use the brands scented for use on babies unless you are trying to appeal to a woman's maternal instincts.

Talcum powder is a good perspiration absorber. Some brands displayed in the cologne section of department stores are loaded with scent. If you use one of these, make sure it contains the same scent as your cologne.

Medicated foot talc is a great way to keep your feet dry, odorless and free from fungus. If your feet have sweat or fungus problems, shake or spray some medicated talc on your feet in the morning and add a little in your shoes before you wear them.

Clean Cotton Clothes

Have you ever smelled your clothes? Other people can. It's a good habit to sniff an article of clothing before wearing it a second time between washes. Of course, there is no reason to stick your nose in your socks, dress shirts and certainly not in your underwear. Imagine getting caught with your nose in your BVDs. You'd probably have to move out of town. Those items of clothing are only good for one wearing between washes. I shouldn't have to mention that, but anyone who has had guys for roommates knows it needs mentioning.

Loose fitting cotton clothes will help you smell your best. Boxers are a little better than briefs because they allow more air to circulate down there. For outerwear, wool is another good choice for avoiding odor in your clothing. Synthetic fabrics have improved in recent years. However, except for the fabrics used in specially designed athletic clothing, synthetics tend to trap moisture and odor more than natural fabrics. A cotton undershirt can protect your dress shirts from perspiration stains as well as odors.

Liquid Lust

Wild boars and other animals excrete a scent or pheromone to get the opposite sex in the mating mood. How would you like to smell like a horny hog? For many years, cologne and aftershave manufacturers have been trying to reproduce the pheromone effect on humans. Looking at the advertisements for cologne, you might think they succeeded. No such luck. Researchers have found certain scents can change a person's mood and even her physiology. Lavender incense, for example, has been found to contribute to a pleasant mood and the smell of phenethyl alcohol can reduce blood pressure. What does this mean for you? Not much. There is no single scent that has been proven to attract all women. A scent that turns one woman on may turn another woman off (although the sweet smell of success seems to have universal appeal). As a rule you can't go wrong with clean and fresh. If you do wear a fragrance, less is best. As I mentioned earlier, women's noses are generally more sensitive than men's noses and it doesn't take much for a manufactured scent to become overpowering.

Men's colognes tend to fall into three categories: citrus, woody or musky. For the clean smell you want during the day, use a small amount of clean-smelling cologne or aftershave with a citrus or woody scent. You can spot these because they are often advertised and marketed with a sports theme. A touch of clean scent can help you freshen up when you don't have time for a shower after a quick workout or a day at work. Save the heavy fragrances for that romantic date or avoid them altogether.

Some men splash aftershave on their face and neck. Don't use both aftershave and cologne unless they are both of the same brand. One fragrance competing with another is a battle of scents you will certainly lose. When it comes to cologne, most guys put a touch or squirt of cologne behind each ear. Other guys put some in the middle of their chest or the sides of their chest below the armpits so the scent filters up through their clothes. The true optimist puts a light touch of cologne a couple inches below the belly button before a big night out. The key is to use only a hint of scent or none at all.

Shopping for a Scent

For the most part, ignore the size of the bottle, the advertising, and the price when shopping for a men's fragrance. Even a small bottle of the right cologne can serve you well for many months. The wrong fragrance will collect dust, or worse, you could actually use the stuff and get a reputation as Pepe Le Pew.

Before you buy cologne, ask at least three attractive women what they prefer to smell on a man. It's a great way to discover what is hot on the market and it's an easy excuse to start up a conversation with a woman you want to meet. The women at the fragrance counter are often hot and they'll be happy to give you some direction about the popular brands. Dakar, Polo Sport by Ralph Lauren and Tommy by Tommy Hilfiger are a few clean-smelling options. Platinum by Chanel is a personal favorite of mine. If you are on a budget, you might want to try Old Spice, which can be purchased in any grocery store. This classic scent reminds some women of their father. Of course, that can be a good thing or a bad thing depending on her relationship with her father.

Before you buy any fragrance, make sure you try at least three types first. Put a suggested scent on the inside of your wrist and wear it for at least ten minutes to find out how it interacts with your body chemistry over time. Keep trying new scents one at a time and get feedback from women until you get the scent that smells good to you and, more important, gets a positive reaction from women. Remember, cologne is free to try and expensive to buy. Some manufacturers offer matching deodorants, talc and even shampoo. Those designer toiletries are expensive, so be choosy. Generally, the deodorants and the shampoos are not worth the money. Talc, cologne, aftershave and even scented hand lotion may be worth the price if you plan to wear more than one product at a time. Gift sets sold around Christmas and Father's Day can make these products more affordable.

Don't be afraid to wear your choice of cologne or aftershave every day. It can become part of your "signature scent." Using a consistent scent offers women a clue that you are not a flaky guy who jumps from one thing to the next. Translation: If you are loyal to a scent, you might be loyal to her.

Care for Skin and Hair

Cut-free Shaving: Using an electric shaver is quicker than shaving properly with a blade and you avoid the problem of facial cuts. However, no matter what the advertisements for electric shavers say, a good shave with a blade is easier on your face and it will make your face feel smoother. If you shave with a blade remember the following steps:

- Keep your whiskers wet with warm water for at least a minute before you start to shave.
- Use a rich shaving cream or lotion or even hair conditioner to lubricate your face better than soap or a light shaving foam.
- Use long steady strokes with a sharp blade following the grain of your beard. Those razors with multiple blades are worth the money because they require fewer strokes that can hack up your skin.
- Rinse the blade with warm water frequently and rinse your face well at the end of the shave.

Check to make sure you don't miss a spot of stubble or shaving cream.

If you still cut yourself, wet a styptic pencil with cold water and apply by pressing against the cut.

If you prefer to use an aftershave, consider a cream or gel to moisturize your face. The alcohol rich aftershaves were more important back in the day of rusty razors and barbershops that used one razor for multiple customers.

HOT TIP

I know guys who swear that the original Afta brand of aftershave has a special effect on the ladies (and it's cheap).

Face Facts

Bar soaps are generally too harsh for your face and they will often leave a layer soap scum that can clog the pores of your skin. Before bed, wash your face with warm water and a gentle cleanser such as Cetaphil that contains sodium lauryl sulfate. After cleansing, lightly pat a thin layer of moisturizer on your face. Be especially gentle with the skin around your eyes. I know moisturizing sounds girly, but consistent use of a good moisturizer will reduce fine lines and wrinkles and help you attract those young supple maidens for many years to come. Your moisturizer should boast antioxidants and you may want to consider applying twice a day during the dry winter months. If you have oily skin, experiment with using a non-alcohol-based astringent and oil-free moisturizer.

Hair Today and Tomorrow

Most hair loss is related to genetics. If baldness runs in your family, testosterone accumulates in the blood vessels leading to the growth area of the hair and kills it. There is little you can do about the problem other than medicines such as Rogaine and Propecia that provide limited results and also carry side effects.

Rogaine is the brand name for Minoxidil. This lotion promotes hair growth in about 25% of men and women and often takes several months to work. New hair is usually thinner and lighter, like baby hair, and grows mostly on the top of the head, not at the hairline. Skin irritation is the most commonly reported side effect. Dizziness and increased heart rate have also been reported and you have to keep using it to maintain results.

Propecia is the brand name for Finasteride. This oral prescription drug inhibits the conversion of testosterone to DHT. Propecia is not effective in men who are completely bald, but it does promote hair growth and slow hair loss in men who are just beginning to lose hair. In one study, 60% of men had new hair growth and more than 80% slowed their hair loss after 6 to 12 months of treatment. Propecia costs about $50 a month and takes at least six months to work, and its long-term safety is unknown. One side effect can be less spark in Little Sparky. But hey, that's why there's Viagra, right?

HOT TIP

In the Los Angeles area there is a clinic that is all the rage with A-list actors who are trying to hold onto their youthful appearance. The Regenix Clinic offers treatments that attempt to stop thinning hair by enhancing the health of your hair and scalp. The process involves scientific analysis of your hair and a personalized program of treatment utilizing topically applied bio-pharmaceuticals. They have a variety of treatments that deal with the factors contributing to hair loss—including genetic predisposition, health, scalp hygiene, and nutrition. Afterwards, additional formulas are used to enhance your existing hair. My uncle is an L.A. actor and he swears by the results, but the treatments are not cheap and Regenix does not promise to cure baldness. If you want information you can call 1-800-REGENIX. No, I don't get a cut. Probably need to work on that.

There are also steps you can take on your own to minimize thinning hair:

Wash your hair regularly with a mild shampoo and minimize the use of styling products near your scalp. An accumulation of dead skin (dandruff), oils, dirt, pollution, and styling products can suffocate the hair follicles.

Wet hair is more prone to breakage, so use your towel to pat dry rather than rubbing dry.

Don't force your hair to go against the grain. Men who wear ponytails or style their hair against the grain encourage premature thinning of their hair because some hair falls out due to the stress on the follicle.

Eat a healthy diet and take a daily multivitamin to make sure your hair gets the protein, vitamins and minerals it needs to stay strong and healthy. Those vitamins will also help keep your skin looking young and lively. Hair loss can be an early sign of illness and malnutrition.

Well, that covers your body. Now, whom your body covers is none of my business.

Chapter 5

THUS CONCLUDING WHY YOU SHOULD SLEEP WITH ME TONIGHT

BRAINS—YOUR MIND IS A TERRIBLE THING TO WASTE

Many people buy into the theory that you are born with a certain IQ and that your IQ determines how smart and successful you will be. What a bunch of dummies! Some people are born with more brainpower than others, but your brain is like a muscle that you can develop and there are many ways to be smart. You may have a knack for mechanical things or you may be good at dealing with people. The key is to exercise your brain by continuously challenging and educating yourself on topics you find interesting and important.

HOT TIP

Taking a college class is a great place to meet young and attractive women, so you can satisfy your sexual appetite while you feed your brain. The coursework is a perfect conversation starter. It helps if you pick a class that will attract a lot of women.

You can also study on your own by reading good books from your local library. I've actually had a couple of cute women approach me in the library while I was doing research for this book. There must be a book written for single women that tells them to approach guys at the library. Whatever. The library is free and a book makes a great conversation piece. Many guys rarely read a book once they leave school. That gives guys who do read books a huge advantage.

Total Recall

Many people say they have a bad memory. Unless they are brain damaged, they probably have a perfect memory with a lousy filing system. There are complete courses available on memory enhancement. I'm going to give you a summary of a couple of popular techniques so you can start applying them today.

Your mind thinks with pictures. The more vividly you see a picture in your mind, the easier it will be to retrieve. You can make an image in your mind more vivid by picturing the colors of the image, interacting with the image, exaggerating the image and using the image in an illogical way. Try this:

Take a moment to picture a teacup.

Now look up and picture a giant white teacup with two bright red stripes as it tilts above your head pouring scalding hot pea soup all over your face.

There is no doubt that the second picture is more vivid and therefore more memorable. That is because you pictured the colors of the teacup (white with two red stripes), you interacted with the image of the teacup (when it tilted over your head and poured scalding hot pea soup on your face), you exaggerated the image (the teacup was giant and the soup scalding) and the image was illogical (giant teacups rarely hover in the air and tilt over to pour out pea soup on someone's head).

There will be times when you will want to memorize a word that is more conceptual than visual. The trick in this situation is to use the sound or sounds of the word to make one or more word pictures. Let's say you want to remember the word "influence:" "in" could be an old country inn with a red vacancy sign out front; "flue" could be a sick person trying to keep a thermometer in his mouth while he's coughing and sneezing; and "ens" almost rhymes with ants. Your mind works best when the vivid pictures are organized. A sick guy tries to get out of the cold by opening the door of an old country inn. The door falls off the hinges and crushes him and millions of ants are released into the cold. The next step is to find a way to hang the new pictures and access the pictures in the proper order. These places are called memory pegs.

A memory peg is something physical that you know so well it's easy to picture in your mind. Parts of your body or items in the rooms of your home can be used as memory pegs. In your home you first picture a room and pick out five distinctive items in the room in a clockwise pattern. You can do this with all the rooms in your house if you have several items to memorize.

Your mind works best when there is a strong link between your memory peg and the picture you are remembering. You make the link stronger by making it colorful, illogical, exaggerated and full of action!

Let's say a clockwise tour of your kitchen would include a table, a refrigerator, a sink, a trashcan and an oven. Here is how you could use these pegs to memorize a shopping list of five items: a dozen eggs, milk, frozen peas, six chicken legs and a bag of potato chips. Picture the table shaking and the tabletop growing in the shape of a giant egg until a giant egg with the number 12 painted in green breaks through the tabletop with a big crashing noise, throwing splinters everywhere. When you open the refrigerator, you see there is nothing inside but a skinny cow embarrassed to be caught, standing inside drinking out of a blue milk carton. When you turn the faucet on the kitchen sink, frozen green peas start shooting out of the faucet and ricocheting off the bottom of the sink in every direction, including your face. You move over to the trashcan and notice a chicken with four legs is dancing like a Russian folk dancer on the trashcan lid. Finally, you open the oven and thousands of potato chips fly out like mini Frisbees. You catch one in your mouth and suddenly your mouth blows up like a balloon. You open your mouth and pull out a big bag of chips. Now, this may sound like a bad acid trip and that's the point. We remember the unusual and forget the ordinary.

You can use these techniques to remember virtually any list. So, at this point you may be thinking, why should I care about memorization? I can write stuff down if I need to remember it. Well, you may not have the opportunity to write down a woman's name when you meet her. And a woman's name is one thing you'll be wise not to forget.

When you meet a woman, ask her name, ask why her parents chose that name, and use it strategically in your conversation with her. Use the sound or sounds of the name to create an exaggerated picture in you mind and then find an absurd way to attach the picture to some feature of her that catches your eye. Let's say her name is Cindy.

1. Break the name into sounds that you can associate with something visual. For example: "sin" and "tea."
2. Think up exaggerated pictures to match the sounds. Flaming red Satan horns could represent sin. Remember that giant teacup we visualized earlier? Of course you do. That could remind you of the word tea.
3. Have the pictures interact with her and each other in an outrageous way. The flaming red Satan horns crack through her skull and stick out from her cute hairstyle that you noticed when you first met her. She screams in pain and then uses her giant teacup to douse the flaming horns with tea. Remembering Cindy's name could be the first step to finding out if she really is horny.

Want another example? You notice Lisa is wearing a white blouse over her beautiful bosoms. A large circular shadow suddenly falls over her blouse and you look up to see a giant leaning (LEE) saw (SUH) falling over on her. The giant leaning saw falls over on her and cuts through that white blouse without touching her skin so that the blouse almost falls off her body, partially exposing those beautiful bosoms. Now that's an image you'll remember! Tip: try not to stare at her bosoms while you're creating this image.

With some practice you can make up these name associations in a couple of seconds. The wilder the associations, the more likely you will remember her name. Play the memory game in your mind while you repeat her name and ask her about her name. Don't worry if the picture doesn't match the name perfectly. It's the process that helps you remember.

Smart Habits

In the Academy Award winning movie "Forrest Gump," the title character was mildly retarded but led an amazing life partly due to his strong character and his many positive actions. A popular line from the movie was "stupid is as stupid does." The movie illustrated that point by showing several examples of highly intelligent people doing dumb things that screwed up their lives. We know this happens in real life just as much as in the movies. It comes down to the fact that your intelligence is not nearly as important as your decisions and your actions when it comes to your future success. We all do stupid things and when they become habits they can be very destructive. Most people find it almost impossible to eliminate a bad habit because human nature abhors a vacuum.

What does that mean? If you want to stop eating sweets you'll find yourself thinking about not eating sweets. Unfortunately your mind focuses on SWEETS. The next thing you know, you've wolfed down a bag of cookies. If you really want to change a habit in your life, you need to focus on what you want to do instead of what you don't want to do. The best way to do that is to trade a bad habit for a better habit. You also need to commit to that new habit for 21 days. Behavior modification experts say 21 days is the amount of time it takes most people to alter a behavior.

If you want to stop eating sweets, prepare a bunch of celery and carrot sticks in a sandwich bag or pack around a protein shake or some nutrition bars and have them handy to eat whenever you are tempted to eat a piece of candy or a cookie.

If you want to stop smoking, make sure you have sugarless gum to pop in your mouth instead.

If you want to stop criticizing people, put a rubber band around your wrist and snap it every time you are about to say something critical. Then find a way to express a sincere compliment instead.

If you are habitually late, buy a good novel to read and promise yourself that you will only read it when you arrive early to an appointment. That way the story becomes a reward for arriving early.

And if you want to stop scratching your balls, find some sexy gal to do if for you.

Chapter 6

EVERY SUCCESSFUL MAN WRITES A "TO DO" LIST

AMBITION—SCORING WITH GOALS

When I was in college studying to be a TV news reporter, the head of the Journalism Department gathered all of the graduating TV journalism students into one room to give us a reality check about our meager chances of getting a coveted on-camera position after college. She noted that the number of people in the room was 32, and based on former graduating classes, statistically only one of us would make it on-camera as a professional TV news reporter or anchor. The room went somberly silent. To cut the stress I raised my hand and said, "Sorry for the rest of you, but that person is going to be me."

Just about everyone in the class laughed. I was far from the smartest or most talented person in that group. But after the session, the head of the Journalism Department pulled me aside and said that I probably would be the person most likely to make it because I had the drive, commitment and confidence to make it happen. In fact, to my knowledge, I am the only person from that group of students who made it on-camera as a professional TV journalist. I won a bunch of awards and had some amazing experiences. I've since moved on to a more rewarding and profitable career that I imagined first as a goal. I also drive the German luxury car that I first listed as a goal and live in a beautiful beach house that I first visualized in detail as a goal. I'm not telling you this to brag–O.K., just a little. The fact is I'm sure you couldn't care less about my success and I've certainly faced more than my share of struggles along the way. Your goals may be bigger than mine and you may have the potential to reach higher than I did. I really hope you do. The first step is to truly buy into this concept of writing down and visualizing your goals. Give the next exercises 100% of your attention and commitment. If you do, I can assure you that the long-term results will be more than worth the effort.

Focus Factor

One day you decide you want to buy a certain car and suddenly you see that type of car everywhere you look. Is it possible those cars were there all the time and you just didn't notice? You are short on cash to buy the car but suddenly opportunities to make more money and acquire financing seem to appear everywhere you look. Is that just a coincidence? The answer to both questions can be found in a concept called "focused awareness." Something special happens when we decide exactly want we want and commit to getting it. Our mind turns into an automatic guidance system to help us bring that goal into our reality. This may sound like some psychological mumbo jumbo, but it's an extremely powerful concept. The first step is to decide exactly what you really want.

Five Steps to Getting Anything You Want

Grab a couple of reliable pens, some paper and a clock. Then find a place where you won't be bothered for at least one hour. If you don't have time for this now, wait until you have the time.

Step 1: At the top of a blank piece of a paper write, "I am." Do the same for three other pages and at the top of each write one of the following: "I do," "I have" and "I give." Fill each page with your hopes and dreams, using the following guidelines:

Write what you want to happen in positive terms. Don't say what you don't want to happen. Be very specific, state your dreams in the present tense and consider the following categories: career, financial, material, relationships, emotional, physical, social. For example: Instead of writing "I want to be rich," write "I have more than one million five hundred thousand dollars in net worth." Instead of writing "I want a pretty girlfriend," write something like "My beautiful, thin, blonde girlfriend is getting in the Jacuzzi with me wearing nothing but a smile." Write quickly and fill the pages. Don't hesitate and don't let reality bog you down. These are your dreams and there is no limit. Start writing now.

Step 2: Look back to your lists and circle five dreams that you would like to turn into a goal. You turn a dream into a goal by deciding that the dream is possible and adding a date of accomplishment. First, number the circled goals in the order of their importance to you. Next, write down your list of top five goals in order with a deadline attached to each goal. Example: I'm traveling through Europe in a limousine and spending my nights in castles on a vacation before my 30th birthday. Do this now.

Step 3: Create a plan for your top five goals by writing down the following:

One step I will take to achieve my goal:

Today—

This week—

This month—

Until I reach my goal—

Next, write a short paragraph about how a person would need to act in order to achieve these goals.

Step 4: Attach more emotion to each of your top five goals by first writing down three examples of what you would regret most about never achieving that goal. If your goal is to meet the woman of your dreams, you could describe the lonely nights and how you would feel about yourself for failing to take action to meet her. You know, pretty much how your life was before you started reading this book. Then, for each of your top five goals, write three reasons you will feel great when you achieve that goal. Focus on your sense of accomplishment and the enjoyment you will get from being with that woman who rocks your world.

Step 5. Picture in your mind achieving each of your five goals and how you will feel to have achieved them. Visualize these experiences with as much detail and positive emotion as you can imagine. If you are picturing the woman you want to meet, picture the color of her hair and the expression on her face. Picture the clothes she is wearing, or not wearing. Picture yourself "interacting" with her. I'll leave that up to your fertile imagination. The more vivid and emotional you make your goals, the more powerful the experience will be in helping to shape your future. Whenever possible, before you go to bed, read your goals, visualize yourself achieving each goal and then visualize yourself celebrating having achieved your goals.

By following these steps daily, your thoughts will direct your subconscious mind to focus like a laser beam on where you need to go and how you will get there. This may seem a bit metaphysical, but it sure works. Reaching your goals will still take decisive actions on your part. But when your goals are clearly defined, the right actions will become much more clear to you. Opportunities will present themselves and there will be times when you will feel like the whole universe is working to help you reach your goals.

When you do achieve one of your goals, check it off and proudly write the word "VICTORY" next to it. Do something special to celebrate the achievement of that goal. Do this for each goal you achieve. You will notice something quite miraculous happens once you start chalking up these successes. You'll find that achieving the goals is not nearly as important as the person you become having achieved them. The sense of accomplishment you achieve will make you more confident, and true confidence is like a magnet for women.

The Truth About Time

We all have the same 24 hours a day to reach our goals. How we choose to use those hours defines our lives. If you are not working to achieve your dreams, you are probably helping someone else achieve his dreams. Working in a dead-end job? You are helping to make the owner of that company rich. Eating the processed food you see advertised on TV? You are ruining your health while enriching the executives and stockholders of those brands, advertising and media companies.

The average man spends much of his time watching TV and working in a job he merely tolerates. The wealthy man devotes his early years to educating himself and acquiring excellence in at least one talent that generates big money. We just introduced you to a time-tested technique for identifying and achieving what you want in your life. Spend your time achieving your goals if you want to avoid a life of regrets, and don't be afraid to take risks. I've interviewed dozens of millionaires. None of them regretted the things they tried and failed. They learned to use each failure as a valuable learning experience and to grow from each experience. The millionaires I interviewed did share one regret. They regretted the risks they didn't take. Women are attracted to goal-oriented men who are willing to take risks to get what they want, so be one of those men.

The ABC's of Time Management

You have to take the time to manage your time but it doesn't have to be complicated or difficult. Simply follow these six steps:

Step 1: Write down any time-specific appointments you have for the day.

Step 2: Write down everything you want to accomplish in a given week. Remember, this list should include some action to bring you closer to achieving one of your major goals. Often it's best to have two lists, one for work and one for your personal life.

Step 3: Write a capital letter A, B or C to the left of each item on your list.

A = very important and very urgent. "A" is for tasks that need to be accomplished today. This includes tasks that take you closer to achieving your most important goals. How do you eat an elephant? One bite at a time. That is how you need to approach your major goals. Budget at least some time each day toward accomplishing your long-term goals and you will eventually achieve them. If one of your long-term goals is to save more money, an "A" task might be to check out a book on saving money from your local library or to create a plan to pay off your debts. If one of your "A" tasks is meeting the woman of your dreams, you may want to write down that you will introduce yourself to at least one beautiful woman that day. Hey, you have to do it if's is on your to-do list.

B = important and somewhat urgent. "B" is for tasks that could be finished tomorrow if necessary.

C = less important and not urgent. "C" tasks can be accomplished later in the week, or the following week. You may decide some "C" tasks are not really worth your time at all.

Step 4: Number each of your A, B and C tasks in order of urgency and priority. For example, your most urgent "A" task would be an "A1" and your most urgent "B" task would be a "B1."

Step 5: Write down your appointments in the order that they occur during the day.

Step 6: Start with your "A1" task and then your "A2" task and work your way down the list of "A" tasks before moving to "B" tasks. Whenever you accomplish a task, cross it out and write a large checkmark or a "V" for victory next to the task. Remember to check your appointments and commit to accomplishing all of your "A" tasks in a given day. If you consistently fail to accomplish some of the "A's," you need to reflect on whether you are being inefficient or whether you are categorizing your tasks incorrectly. The next day you can again prioritize your old tasks and include new tasks that must be completed. You can use this system easily on a PDA, such as a Palm Pilot, and the device will even remind you when you have appointments. To think we used to call a guy a palm pilot when he played with his joystick too much.

Chapter 7

LET ME GET THAT FOR YOU

COMMITMENT— HOW GOOD GUYS FINISH FIRST

Many guys don't open doors for women anymore. They have no idea how many doors they are closing for themselves. The radical feminist movement has spent the last 40 years trying to convince us that men and women are the same and should be treated the same. If they want to pee standing up, that's their business. Most women today want equal opportunities and equal pay, but they still appreciate that rare gentleman who treats them like a princess. Polite gestures make a woman feel cared for and help her to appreciate you. That is just one reason you should open doors and more:

- When a woman drops something, be the first to pick it up.
- If a woman shivers or mentions that she is cold, offer her your coat.
- Help a woman on with her coat.
- Carry your umbrella over a woman so she doesn't get wet in the rain.
- If a woman is getting harassed, pretend to be her boyfriend until the guy moves on.
- If a woman doesn't have the exact change for a purchase, offer some of your own.
- If you are both smokers, offer her a cigarette and a light.
- Hail her a taxi and offer to share or pay the fare.
- Stand when a woman approaches your table or when you are being introduced.
- Remain standing until all women at a table are seated.
- If the opportunity arises to kiss a woman's hand, don't raise her hand up to your lips, rather lower your lips down to her outstretched hand.

Simple gestures like these are a great way to stand out from the crowd and make a good impression. They also serve as a suave technique for making that initial contact with a woman you want to meet. Make sure you spread this gentleman stuff around to women of all shapes, sizes and ages. The woman getting the attention won't be the only person who notices. Every woman within eyeshot will rank you higher on her good guy scale. You'll be surprised at the positive reactions you get from women when you start to act like a real gentleman. And, this may sound hokey, but you'll be amazed at how great it makes you feel as a man.

The Power of a Promise Kept

A woman knows that a man will say almost anything to get her into bed. They look beyond his words to see if he is the kind of guy who will stick around after the first night of passion. One way a woman judges a man's intentions is to pay close attention to whether he keeps his promises to her and to others. When you ask for her number and wait to call until a week later, you are breaking a commitment because in her mind you should have called sooner. If you show up late to meet her, you have broken a commitment to be there when you said you would. If you have been divorced or you slept around before you met her, she'll probably need extra assurance that you have developed the character to commit to a future relationship down the road.

There are many ways that you can show a woman that you are a man of character with the ability to keep commitments. Simply caring for your pet or keeping houseplants alive in your home demonstrates this quality. The definition of a bachelor's apartment: all the houseplants are dead but there's something growing in the refrigerator. Close ties with your family and friends will also score points with a woman on her commitment scale. That doesn't mean women like mamma's boys, but when they see you display care and affection toward your family, they are more likely to see you as a person who will be caring toward them. Prove to her that you are reliable by keeping small commitments and she will begin to trust you much sooner.

The Eyes Have It

Some guys think they need to be cool and aloof to attract women. This is far from the case. Scanning the room for other women or looking off like you don't care about her will make a woman feel anxious and less attracted to you. A woman wants to know that you are interested and she instinctively knows that successful men go after and focus on what they want. If you really like a woman, you need to let her know it by looking into her eyes and paying attention to her as if she is the only person in the room.

Listen Your Way to Her Heart

One of the biggest complaints women have about men is that they don't truly listen. Men often feel the need to brag about their accomplishments to try to impress a woman, but too much bragging usually has the opposite effect. Women tend to be more active in their listening than men and they appreciate it when men use the techniques of active listening. You accomplish this by leaning toward her, nodding and affirming verbally while you are listening to her. You also want to keep the conversation moving with open-ended questions about the topic she is discussing along with positive reinforcement about what she is saying. She wants you to respect her opinion and to search out areas that the two of you do have in common. Think of it as intelligence gathering. In the next chapters you'll learn how to use the information from all this active listing to your advantage.

Chapter 8

GIRL SAYS, "I LIKE YOU, BUT I'M"JUST NOT SURE YOU'RE MY TYPE

COMPATIBILITY—CREATING THE CONNECTION

An attractive and successful business executive hits on a young party girl in a bar and she blows him off to leave with one of the waiters. No reason to be shocked. It's possible that the girl waits tables herself and feels more comfortable with the hired help. When you have nothing in common with a woman, she is probably not worth your time, no matter how beautiful she might be. One of the easiest ways to build rapport with a woman is to find out what the two of you do have in common and focus on those commonalities when you talk to her. We are naturally drawn to other people with common interests, beliefs and experiences. That doesn't mean you have to agree with everything she says. You may both enjoy arguing. This is not what I would choose to have in common with someone, but it seems to work for some couples. Probably it has something to do with great make-up sex.

When you are searching for that common connection, start with your ears. Weave questions into your conversation to find out what she likes and then truly listen. Avoid talking about yourself unless it relates to what she is saying. Be careful about what you do say about yourself to make sure it's positive and brief. She is bound to enjoy the conversation more if it revolves around her. That doesn't mean you interrogate her. When you ask a question, pause for her answer and share your positive thoughts about it as well as any common feelings you may have. She'll notice that you're a good listener who is interested in more than her body. That will make her more interested in sharing her body with you!

The Mirror Miracle

People already use this technique subconsciously. When two people are communicating in sync you will notice they start to speak with similar pacing and use similar gestures. You can jumpstart this process consciously by subtly mirroring a woman's speaking style and mannerisms. If she gestures with her right arm when she talks, you gesture in a similar way with your left arm when you begin to speak. Notice I said her right arm and your left arm. That way the same side is gesturing, just like when you gesture at a mirror. If she pauses before speaking, you do the same. If she slouches in her chair, slouch a little yourself. If she adjusts her bra strap, you adjust your…never mind. Don't make your mirroring obvious. You don't have to mirror everything she does. Subtle mirroring will make her feel like you understand her and relate to her. It also requires that you pay more thorough attention to her than you might otherwise.

You can use this technique whenever you are trying to build rapport with another person. It may sound manipulative but it's actually a compliment. You are showing the woman that you are willing to get in sync with her perspective and style. If you are careful and very subtle, she'll never notice that you are mirroring her. She'll just feel a common connection between the two of you. She should. You created it.

The Magic Word

There is one word that is precious to every woman. It sounds beautiful to her. It gets her attention and you better not forget it. That magic word is her name. In Chapter 5 I gave you some powerful tips for how to memorize a woman's name in a matter of seconds. Once you know her name and the story behind her name, you have gained some vital information about her. Say her name only during key points in the conversation when you really want to get her attention or you are about to ask her an important question. Use her name carefully and strategically like the magic word that it is.

The Right Touch

Never underestimate the power of a touch. When a woman casually touches a man on the hand or arm, it's a powerful clue that should not be ignored. If a woman touches you, take that as a green light that she is interested. Look for an opportunity to softly touch her back or respond in some other affectionate way. You rarely want to initiate a touch when you first meet a woman. Coming from a guy, touching can be interpreted as aggressive and forward. It's better to wait until you are confident that you have built rapport with her and even then touch her softly, non-sexually and only briefly. Rotating her breasts like radio knobs and saying, "Come in, Rangoon" should wait until the second date…at least.

When you do touch a woman for the first time, you can make it memorable by touching her clothing or skin very softly. To understand the amount of pressure, try gliding your fingers from one hand over the back and wrist of your other hand. When the touch is light enough to make your skin tingle, you've got it just right. You can stop touching yourself now. It's very important that your initial touch is non-sexual. Lightly touching her upper arm or lower back to help guide her through a crowd is the caring type of touch that women appreciate. A soft touch to her finger or wrist as you admire a piece of jewelry is also effective. Brushing her hair out of her face is a little forward if used too soon, but this type of touching also fits into the non-sexual category. It's even possible to create the intimacy of a touch without actually touching by drinking out of the same glass. You can accomplish this by ordering an exotic drink and having her taste it.

The Key to Charisma

The ability to make another person feel compatible to you and drawn to you is one of the most powerful skills you can ever learn. The king of charisma is probably former President Bill Clinton. He could have a meeting with his worst enemy and that person would walk out of the meeting feeling truly heard and appreciated.

Charisma is about welcoming people in rather than pushing them away. It's a way of looking at the world and other people. If you have a "me vs. them" attitude and you are judgmental of others, you put up a barrier around yourself even when you don't mean to. That's one reason many guys get so nervous around beautiful women. They judge these women as different and superior to them. Charisma comes from an "us" mentality. It comes from realizing that we are all human beings and we all have roughly the same needs and insecurities. It means being friendly and truly interested in getting to know the other person, whether she's a little old lady who lives down the street or an underwear model who rarely wears underwear.

Chapter 9

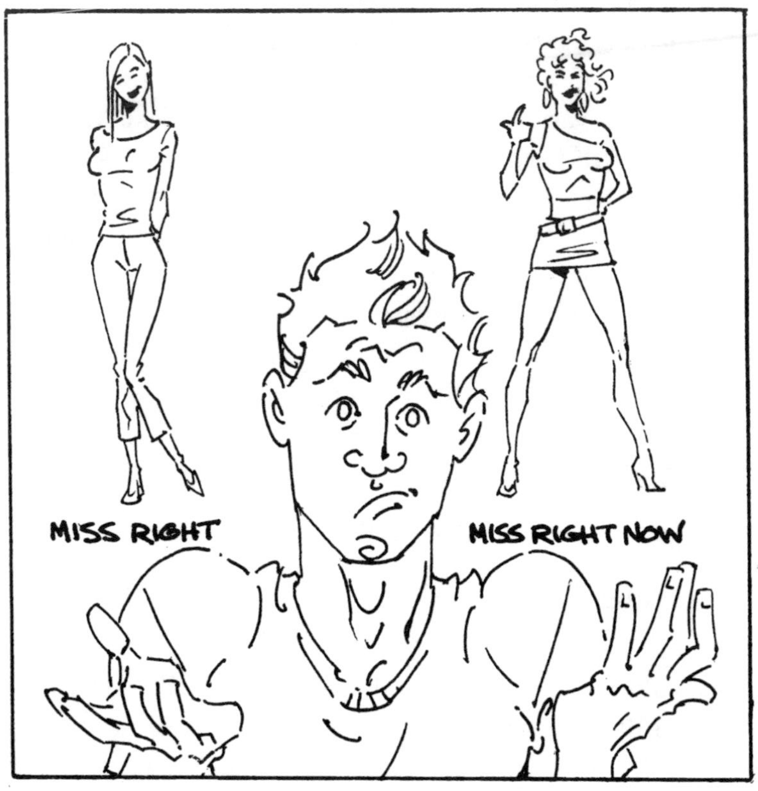

I JUST CAN'T DECIDE!

WINNING THE NUMBERS GAME

Do you want a relationship or someone to suck face with? The "girl next door" or a "bar babe" in a leather miniskirt? Looking for all of the above? Well, at least you have options. But a guy has problems if he keeps trying to build relationships with bar babes who think spending the night is a long-term commitment. Deciding what you really want in a woman will save you time, money and a lot of hassles.

Are you looking for?

A variety of women

A relationship with the right woman

A variety of women until the right one comes along

If you want a variety of women, watch out for jealous husbands and protect yourself from those nasty diseases passing between people these days. Remember, a one-night stand is always a risk. These days, without protection, sleeping around is less a game of conquest and more like a game of Russian roulette.

If you want a relationship with the right woman, check out the section about online dating later in this chapter and read what I have to say about the website eHarmony.com.

Every night I had a strange girl. Same girl — she was just strange.

– Michael Davis

Know What You Want

Most guys want to find the right woman, but they don't mind a few distractions along the way. The following survey will help you focus your search. Fill in the spaces and circle any characteristics that apply. A free copy of this survey with spaces for your answers is available for you at www.singleguysurvival.com.

Physical:

The woman I want should be at an age between (youngest age) and (oldest age). Her ideal race would be (preferred race) or (second choice /any).

Her body style is (thin, petite, athletic, big booty, big breasted, curvy). Her height should be between shortest height) and (tallest height). The hair color and style I prefer is (blonde, brunette, black, redhead, long, short, straight, curly).

Personality:

Her image is (sophisticated, outdoorsy, party girl, girl next door, artsy, earthy, ambitious, sexy). Emotionally, she is (sensitive, caring, loving, cheery, serious, spontaneous, outgoing, shy, like mother).

Status:

When it comes to education I expect her to be a (college graduate, trade school graduate, high school graduate, able to spell her name).

Her job status is (student, homemaker, blue collar, trade, professional, successful enough to support me in the manner to which I have become accustomed).

She is a (practicing, non-practicing Protestant, Catholic, Jew, Muslim, Buddhist, Agnostic, Atheist, Hare Krishna with a habit of hanging out in airport terminals).

I expect her marital status to be (single, without kids, divorced O.K., widowed O.K., with kids O.K., married to a Hell's Angel).

Hobbies and Habits:

Recreational activities she should enjoy or at least tolerate are (camping, tennis, watching sports, hunting, fishing, golf, shopping, boating, skiing, movies, reading, dancing, travel, dining out, sex with circus animals).

She should be willing to tolerate the following habits: (light smoking, heavy smoking, light drinking, heavy drinking, illegal drugs, lateness, messiness, lack of organization, perfectionism, laziness, procrastination, workaholic, farting in public). By the way, if you circle more than three of these items it's time for some serious self-evaluation!

Use your answers from the worksheet to describe your ideal woman on a sheet of paper. At the top of the paper write: My Ideal Woman… Feel free to add any additional characteristics that are important to you. Do it now.

Get What You Need

While it's good to know what you want in a woman, some qualities are more important to you than others. Pick five characteristics from your list that you feel your ideal woman must possess. At this point her hair color may not be as important as other qualities. Then again, maybe that is important to you. Take out another piece of paper and write at the top: The woman in my life must… and then write down her "must have" qualities.

Once you have written down your "must have" list, never settle for a woman who doesn't offer those qualities. There are too many wonderful women out there for you to waste your time on those who can never give you what you need.

These exercises are vital because the law of focused awareness will help you find your ideal woman once you have identified her on paper. Remember the law of focused awareness from Chapter 7? Once you clearly identify and write down the qualities you "must have" in a woman, read through the qualities occasionally before you go to sleep. Your subconscious will work like a tracking beam to help you find her. By the way, you probably want to keep these lists private, especially from the women you date.

Now that you have determined the qualities you want and the qualities you need in a woman, picture her in your mind. Think about what she looks like, how she dresses and how she carries herself. Picture her in as much detail as possible. Now think about the kind of man you will have to become to attract that woman. How should you carry yourself? How should you dress? How should you treat her? You can use this book as the roadmap to become that guy. If you can see it, you can be it, my friend.

The question you have to ask yourself is "Am I committed to do what it takes to attract the woman of my dreams?" That doesn't mean you have to be great looking or filthy rich or pretend to be someone you're not. Most women can spot a phony. They really just want a good guy who will treat them well. You need to accentuate your good qualities and help women associate their feelings of love and romance with you. Once you master this concept, it's simply a matter of choosing the woman who best embodies your desires and needs.

Single!

When you know what you want in a woman, where do you look? Just about everywhere but the men's room. Some single guys say they can't meet women because they're not into the bar scene. If you feel that way, then you'll prove yourself right. I've picked up some beautiful women in bars and I met my wife in a bar, but bars and nightclubs are not the only places to meet women. The key is to find opportunities wherever you go. Make it a part of your daily routine. Shop around and play the numbers game—to win.

If you've ever gone snow skiing, you know that people skiing solo move into a special lift line and call out "single!" until another single hops in line with them. This is a great way to meet new people because you are letting others know you're single. The idea works just as well when there is no lift line in sight. One of the easiest ways to find single women is to allow your friends and relatives to do the looking for you. When successful couples are surveyed about how they met, a large percentage met through friends or relatives. Simply let a few key people know that you are available to meet new women who might be your type. It will help your cause greatly if you casually mention some of the characteristics on your "must have" list as qualities you are looking for in a potential date (without telling them you have a "must have" list).

Your friends can set up a casual introduction or invite you both to a party with other friends. Avoid couples-only gatherings, though, because that puts far too much pressure on both of you. If your friends insist on a blind date, make it a quick lunch or suggest the two of you get acquainted over a glass of wine or a cup of coffee. You can always set up another date if you two hit it off. There are few experiences worse than a long and expensive "Blind Date from Hell."

Online Personals

Beautiful women are now just a click away, thanks to the Internet. No, I'm not talking about those porn sites on your "favorites" list. Online dating sites have become mainstream, with millions of visitors each month. Some of the most popular sites include match.com, matchmaker.com and date.com. It doesn't cost anything to check out photos of the women on some of these sites and the cost of signing up is usually only \$20-\$30 a month. You'll probably be shocked to find there are attractive women in your area who have posted their profiles on these sites. Because some women are hesitant to post an online personal, you may want to post your own profile. Here are some tips to maximize the results of your online dating:

- Submit a professional photograph that makes you look your best. It helps to have your picture taken in high-status clothes in front of an impressive backdrop such as a famous resort, an impressive landmark or a nice country club setting.

- Let your photos do the talking. Don't be too specific about your likes and dislikes. A little mystery will greatly increase the number and quality of responses from eligible women.

- When you do talk about yourself, remember that women are looking for the seven qualities of the Modern Alpha Male. When asked about yourself, subtly and briefly describe ways that you excel in at least some of these qualities.

- Make sure you ask for a photo and converse with the person by email or over the phone before you set a face-to-face date.

- When women respond, you should ask a lot of questions if you don't want to get involved with somebody's wife. Surveys have found that more than 20% of the people who respond to online personals are married.

If you are more interested in a mate than a date, you may want to try eHarmony.com. eHarmony.com is helping more couples get married than a drive-through chapel in Vegas. Each new eHarmony.com user fills out a long relationship questionnaire developed by Ph.D. psychologists that is designed to identify a person's key characteristics, beliefs, values, emotional health and skills. eHarmony.com digs deeply into the important aspects of personality that influence our romantic relationships, providing a comprehensive profile for each user. Once the profile is complete, eHarmony matches people based on 29 key dimensions to encourage compatibility and relationship success. It is really a high-tech throwback of the matchmakers from the past but it seems to be working.

Join the Joiners

Another great way to meet women is to join groups and group activities. People who get out and get involved tend to be a lot more fun than your average homebody. Not only will you meet quality women, you also may learn something and enjoy yourself in the process. Here are some great group activities for meeting women:

- Fitness classes such as Yoga, Pilates and Aerobics are packed with healthy women interested in looking and feeling their best. You'll be outnumbered!

- Coed sports such as softball, tennis, golf, volleyball, and martial arts training provide many opportunities to interact with sporty women. If you don't spot a prospective date in one group, don't hesitate to quit and join another.

- College classes such as dancing, creative writing, art, self-defense and physical education are packed with attractive women. Don't rule out a massage class if you are looking for a deep physical relationship or just some new moves to add to your repertoire. Once again, there is no law that says you have to stay in the class if you don't see any women who fit into your private study group.

- Group trips put on by recreation departments, churches and community colleges offer a variety of getaways. Water and snow skiing, camping, hiking, biking, tours, cruises, and concerts offer plenty of chances for interaction.

- Church or temple is a great place to find single women looking for a spiritual as well as a physical connection. Don't think all women who go to church are prudes. Where else are they going to go to confess their sins of the flesh? A larger organization with specific programs for your age group will provide the most opportunities.

- Political or community organizations. You might be surprised by the women you meet in these organizations. Women passionate enough to fight for a cause will have plenty of passion left over for the bedroom. I know guys who troll liberal rallies (anti-war, animal rights, etc.) looking for sexy hippie chicks who still believe in free love. Of course it helps if you actually believe in the liberal cause and you may have to put up with armpit hair.

Generally there is no need to be "on the prowl" when you participate in group activities. Just make sure you take advantage of the opportunities available to interact with the women who interest you. The organization or activity becomes an easy topic of conversation and you'll get plenty of chances to ask women out.

When "No" Is No Big Deal

If a woman says "no" when you are reaching down to remove her panties, it should set off buzzers and flashing lights in your head. At that stage of the game, no absolutely means no. Halt and retreat immediately. But the mating dance has many stages. Early in the dance, no might mean maybe. One night in a fancy nightclub in Guadalajara, Mexico, I asked a beautiful Mexican girl to dance. She smiled but politely said no, so I started to walk away. Another beautiful girl stopped me and criticized me for being ignorant about Mexican culture. When I asked what she meant, I was invited to join both girls for an education that really helped me succeed south of the border (if you know what I mean). It turns out the girls were sisters and they sat me down to watch how the Mexican guys asked women to dance as many as four to five times before finally giving up. The sisters told me that a Mexican woman is almost obligated to say no at least once to present a challenge to the man. That got me thinking about how I must have been letting opportunities slip by up in the States as well.

Nobody wants to hear "no." The fear of rejection can be paralyzing for many guys. They picture the worst possible outcome and see themselves being humiliated. This self-imposed fear makes many guys act hesitantly and awkwardly. Women pick up on these submissive mannerisms and instinctively reject these guys. Women can sense that the stakes are high for these guys. They don't want to be the source of crushing their fragile egos, so they cut them off at the pass.

The Modern Alpha Male understands that rejection is really an illusion. If he approaches a woman and she turns him down, he really hasn't lost anything. He wasn't with her before and he isn't with her now. He realizes that even the greatest batters strike out at least twice for every hit, and they get at least three swings every time they step up to the plate. The Modern Alpha Male knows that it is his job to pursue women. The women's job is to accept or reject his advances. Sometimes a woman will play hard to get simply to test the guy's ambition and persistence. Early in the meeting process, an ambiguous "no" may mean "not yet." A Modern Alpha Male will simply shrug it off and try another approach.

Even if the no is definite, he knows there are thousands of reasons that a woman may reject a guy during the meeting process. She may have a boyfriend, or maybe she recently got dumped. She may be in a bad mood, or she may have a feminine problem. She may like small skinny guys and he happens to be big and muscular. The list is endless. A Modern Alpha Male appreciates a firm early "no" because that way he can move on to another woman without wasting too much time and energy. It is, after all, her loss for missing out on everything you have to offer. You do have great stuff to offer, right? You sure will if you put this book into practice. The Modern Alpha Male knows that it is not only his job to initiate the first step but also virtually every step thereafter. He makes the approach and keeps the conversation rolling. He makes the phone call and he happily calls back if she fails to return the call. He asks for the date and he initiates the first kiss.

Some guys resent that they have to put their ass on the line at every stage of the mating dance, but the Modern Alpha Male knows that initiating each step gives him much of the power. He gets to approach any woman he wants and he gets to talk to her and date her on his timeline. It's a numbers game and it's a game you can win. A guy who plays the numbers game knows that he may flirt with nine women for every one woman who goes out with him. On average he can expect a sexual encounter with only one out of three of the women who go out with him, and that may take three dates. That means a typical guy can expect to flirt with as many as 27 women and go on as many as nine dates for each successful seduction. Don't like those odds? You can always find a sure thing inside a bottle of hand lotion.

I know you are probably thinking, "I don't have time for all that!" The truth is that you can trim these numbers dramatically with some technique and experience. Even then, you will want to date several women at one time. Let me repeat that. You will date several women at one time. This important practice not only saves time, it makes you more effective with every woman you date. When a guy dates only one woman it makes him overly sensitive to how she reacts toward him. She may be moody, she may get into a small argument with him or she may feel he is being too pushy for sex. The guy will naturally be more dependent on her and he's more susceptible to a blow to his confidence if things don't work out. Think of it as driving down a rocky road without a spare tire. If you are pursuing more than one woman at a time you'll always know that you have a backup so you'll be less likely to get worked up if one relationship starts to go flat. Also, you'll naturally have a more relaxed attitude that will be more attractive to all the women you date. You'll also tend to be less pushy regarding sex because you'll always have another babe as backup. Imagine the possibilities! How are you going to talk all these beautiful women into going out with you? I'm so glad you asked.

Chapter 10

FINALLY, A GUY WHO KNOWS HOW TO PICK UP A WOMAN!

THE ULTIMATE PICK-UP STRATEGY

Girls are much more psychic than guys. They're the first to know if you're going to get laid.

– Paul Rodriquez

Maybe you're too busy to take classes or join a bunch of groups. Maybe you don't trust your friends and relatives to fix you up. Maybe Internet personals seem too impersonal. There is always the direct approach to meeting women. If you've read Chapters 2 through 8, you've already learned how to transform yourself into a chick magnet by enhancing the qualities of the Modern Alpha Male. This will make your job a lot easier when you go out to meet women. What you say is less important than how you say it and what you bring to the table when you're saying it. But you still need to say something and it better not be some lame pick-up line.

You've probably noticed that some guys seem to have a knack for meeting women. Chances are they've stumbled on to a few techniques of "The Ultimate Pick-up Strategy." This strategy is the product of years of research and experimentation. Numerous men have risked embarrassment and rejection perfecting these techniques. The strategy is never to be used for evil pursuits. Only he of pure intentions—O.K., O.K., enough hype. When you call something "the ultimate," you have to milk it for all it's worth. The Ultimate Pick-up Strategy involves five steps:

Step 1: The Prep

Picking up a woman was pretty straightforward back in the Stone Age. A guy spotted an attractive female, clubbed her over the head, and dragged her back to his cave. Sure the process might require the massacre of her protective family members. But a good head-clubber could pretty much have his pick of cave babes. What happens today? A guy spots a beautiful woman and his body shifts back into caveman mode. His senses intensify, his heart starts to race, and his ability to speak becomes reduced to grunts or the modern equivalent of, "Hey baby, what's your sign?" A guy's physiological response to the opposite sex comes right out of those Stone Age days. Modern men must control these caveman urges. Go around clubbing women and you could be arrested. These days you have to knock her out with your confidence and style.

The first priority is to get in the right place mentally and emotionally. Every successful action starts as a successful thought. The Modern Alpha Male knows that if he wants positive results, he first needs to prime the pump with positive thoughts. The two tried-and-true techniques for preparing your mind for success in any endeavor are visualization and positive self-talk. The purpose of these techniques is to practice mentally the positive behavior and to block out the negative thoughts that tend to pop into our heads in stressful situations. We covered these techniques in detail in Chapter 3. Now we will apply them to meeting women.

The first step is to picture flawlessly executing a successful pick-up, and then celebrating when the woman responds as desired. Make the picture in your mind as detailed and vivid as possible and allow yourself to feel the thrill of success. Self-talk can be equally effective. You simply repeat one or two positive phrases over and over again. Mohammad Ali shared his positive self-talk with the world when, before a big fight, he yelled at the top of his lungs, "I am the greatest!" Back in Chapter 3 I told you about my friend Tim who silently repeated, "I'm the best looking guy in the room" and, "All the women want to meet me." Pick a phrase that works for you. Just make sure it's stated in the positive and that you repeat it in your mind with emotion.

After you picture yourself meeting the woman and you've successfully pumped yourself up with positive self-talk, repeat another positive phrase. A phrase I find especially effective when meeting women is short and sweet, but don't underestimate its power to help you get great results with women. The phrase is simply "I like her." Repeat the phrase over and over again before and during the moment you first meet her. The power of this phrase is that your mind only has the ability to focus on one thought at a time. When you think "I like her" over and over again, that thought takes the place of any negative thoughts that might normally run through your mind such as: "There is no way she'd like a guy like me." Or "I'm going to make a fool of myself if I try to talk to her." Those negative thoughts expose themselves through submissive body language and subtly frightened facial expressions.

Aggressive thoughts, such as: "I want her," "I have to have her" or "I've got to add those panties to my collection" can be just as harmful because they cause your face and body language to take on subtle predatory characteristics that frighten some women. Your breathing becomes shallow, your eyes grow intense and your mouth starts to salivate like a wolf stalking a lamb. Save those thoughts for later as she pulls her top over her head. When you are in the initial meeting stage and you continuously repeat the words "I like her," your manner will be more relaxed and friendly. You'll find your body language and smile become more open and confident. This approach will make anyone feel more comfortable around you, especially a beautiful woman who is trying to avoid losers and lechers. You may be those things, but does she have to find out so soon?

Step 2: The Look

Eye contact is very important when you are meeting a woman. You've got to learn how to give it and how to read it. Never stare. That will freak her out. Instead, casually scan the room and pause to glance in her direction for a couple of seconds. You may have to repeat this a few times until you catch her eye. When you do, control the urge to suddenly shift your eyes away. Instead, smile to acknowledge her in a relaxed manner. Despite what the feminist movement and the harbingers of political correctness may try to shove down society's throat, there is nothing wrong with catching a woman's eye and admiring her beauty. Think about how James Bond catches the eye of a woman and model that look. This approach shows you are a confident and dominant male who is obviously interested but not intimidated by her. At this point she may appear a bit startled and turn her eyes away. Don't worry. Looking down or away is a natural submissive reaction for a woman. That is an appropriate response from her in this stage of the mating dance. At this point you can shift your eyes away for a moment before catching her eye a second time. If she peeks back and cocks her head, smiles fully, runs her fingers through her hair, faces her body toward you, arches her back or touches her neck or chest, it's a fair bet that she is interested. If she does any of these things it's time to make your approach. If she doesn't do any of these things, it's still time to make your approach.

HOT TIP

Don't wait too long to make your approach to a beautiful woman. While you're waiting for the right moment to make good eye contact, another guy could be swooping in. Remember, the early bird buries the worm.

Step 3: The Anti-Line

Let's face facts. Starting a conversation with a beautiful woman takes guts. Fortunately, it's a lot easier for a guy who has developed the qualities of the Modern Alpha Male. Single women want to meet guys as much as we want to meet them. However, they must balance this desire with the need to protect their safety and increase their own desirability by presenting a challenge. Women have learned from experience that men need a challenge. Approach her with a smile and allow her to give you some kind of verbal or nonverbal permission to come closer. A simple smile from her is all the permission you need to sit next to her or otherwise enter her comfort zone.

We've all heard the cliché pick-up lines. These infamous lines routinely fail because they come across as forced and insincere. Men think up catchy lines in an attempt to be funny and remove some of the vulnerability of a sincere introduction. Women think up catchy responses to make them pay for their foolishness.

Haven't we met somewhere before?
I work at a V.D. clinic. That must have been it.
Yes. That's why I don't go there anymore.

Hey, baby, what's your sign?
It's a stop sign. Please stop.

Would you like to go outside for some air?
What are we breathing in here?
No. You go. I like the air in here just fine.

I'm been watching you all night. You are the most beautiful girl in the room.
Thanks. Now please go stalk someone else.

What's a nice girl like you doing in a place like this?
Looking for some privacy.

If I told you that you have a beautiful body, would you hold it against me?
If I told you goodbye, would you leave?

The following lines are so bad that a response from the woman is simply not necessary. Most women will just groan and walk away. On the other hand, once you start talking to a woman you can ask her about the worst pick-up line she's ever heard. If she asks for an example from you, you'll have some classics to share:

> Is your father a thief?
> I was just wondering who stole all the stars from the sky and put them in your eyes.
>
> That dress is beautiful. It would look great crumpled on my bedroom floor.
>
> (Softly grabbing her elbow and holding it up) Hey, what's a nice joint like this doing on a girl like you?
>
> This face leaves in an hour—be on it.
>
> I'm not Fred Flintstone, but I can sure make your bed rock.
>
> I'd love to kiss your navel—from the inside.

Yeah, these lines are fun, but when you first approach a woman, you want to avoid these and other pick-up lines at all costs. As Ursula Lindstrom writes in her book *10 Secrets for Success with Beautiful Women* the number one goal of your approach is to come across as both harmless and interested. That means what you say should be subtle and unrehearsed. This approach is almost the opposite of the cliché opening lines that most guys use. That's why I call our approach the Anti-Line. Even the best line is merely a foot in the door. Your objective is to approach her in a friendly and non-threatening manner. What you say and do after that is much more important.

Still, you have to say something when you first meet a woman. Anti-Lines fall into six general categories. Generally, you'll be using a combination of Anti-Lines when you approach a woman. Your job is to put these Anti-Lines into your own words and modify the approach based on the situation and what works best with your personality.

The Diversion:

When a man approaches a woman for the first time, it can be exciting but also a little unnerving for both parties. You can minimize this first moment of nervousness by helping her to focus on something else to divert her attention away from you during that first moment of contact. This approach works best in a crowded area like a nightclub where people are obviously there to meet the opposite sex. This Anti-Line is nothing more than small talk that people use every day to start conversations. There is minimal risk to this approach because you are just being a friendly guy and no one is put on the spot. If she doesn't respond, no harm done.

"This is a great band. I don't think I've ever heard them before. Have you?"

"This place is wild. I had no idea it was so much fun. (pause for her to answer) Is this your first time here?"

"Wow, what a strong drink. How is yours?" (pause for her to answer) These (name of drink) sure pack a punch. What are you drinking?"

"It's a beautiful day out. You seem to be enjoying it."

The Compliment:

We all like to hear nice things about ourselves and women are no exception. The trouble is that a man tends to fixate on a woman's sexual features when he approaches her because that is what attracted him in the first place. Complimenting a woman's legs, butt or breasts is rarely a good opening approach and it will get you nowhere to compliment a woman's hair if your eyes are glued to her breasts. If the woman is drop dead gorgeous, avoid complimenting her looks at all unless you can pick out something obscure like her hands or her shoes. Chances are good that in the past few hours she has already had half a dozen guys tell her that she's beautiful. The best time to use the compliment approach is when a woman seems a bit shy or insecure. Whether she is a nine or just an intriguing seven, try to find something non-sexual and unique to compliment her about and say it in a nonchalant manner as if it were a casual observation.

"You have a sweet smile. I heard only truly sincere people show their bottom teeth when they smile. Do you think that's true?"

"I've never seen a pendant like the one you are wearing. Where did you get it?"

"You are a good dancer. Where did you learn to move like that?" or "I wish I could learn to dance like that."

The Question:

As you may have noticed, many of these Anti-Line examples include a question. Any time you approach a woman you will be asking her questions and pausing to get her involved in the conversation. Sometimes the question may be the first thing you say to her. Any question will do as an opener but the best questions are open-ended, which means they call for more than a yes or no answer. The key is to actually listen to her answer so that you can respond appropriately. One of women's biggest complaints about men is that men don't listen.

Directions—"I think I may be a little lost. Could you tell me how to get to ________?" (pause) "Are there any restaurants in the area that you could recommend?"

"Thanks, my name is ____________. What's yours?" (pause) "How long have you lived around here?

Your environment—"What do you think of this band? Is this your kind of music?"

"What do you think about this place? They seem to make a pretty good drink."

"Have you ever been anywhere with a better view?"

If a woman is writing something or typing on a laptop you can try this question: "Are you a writer?" Many bright women think of themselves as aspiring writers even if they don't make a living at it. She will probably be flattered and you can follow up by asking what she is writing.

The Grand Gesture:

Gallantry is so rare these days that it can make a powerful first impression on a woman. You have to be creative and keep your eyes open for these opportunities. In Chapter 7, "How Good Guys Finish First," I offered dozens of suggestions for actions you can take to make a woman feel special. Buying a drink for a woman or her whole group is a common Grand Gesture. It works best when you are casual about the gesture even though it may be somewhat extravagant. It's important to remember that the drink, appetizer or flower is a gift. You are not buying her time. Wait for her to welcome you over for a conversation.

Of course, a Grand Gesture doesn't have to cost money. If you see an attractive woman shivering, offer her your coat. Even if she doesn't accept, you've started a conversation with her. She may even accept the coat later, once she gets to know you better.

If an attractive woman drops something, be the first to help her pick it up. If her car is broken, help her get it fixed. The opportunities are endless if you keep your eyes open for them.

The Gimmick:

The gimmick approach generally takes some forethought but the opportunities make it worthwhile.

Crossword puzzle—This approach works best in a quiet and relaxed setting with a woman who seems somewhat educated. Sit near the woman you want to approach and work on a crossword puzzle from the newspaper. Leave some of the easier answers blank and begin to act frustrated on an answer. Try to catch her eye or walk over and ask for help on one of the questions. If she has trouble, make your way down to one of the easier answers until you are successfully filling in the crossword puzzle together.

Costume—It doesn't have to be Halloween for you to pull out a costume. The costume works great at a party or a packed bar or nightclub. It also helps if you have a group of friends around to back you up. Dress up in an outrageous getup that makes you easily approachable. Dressing like a pirate, a soldier or something equally macho tends to make you less approachable. A furry animal outfit (with your face showing), a toga or a dress will make you come across more vulnerable, and therefore more approachable to women. Be careful with the dress though. If you look too good, you might get attention you weren't counting on. It helps if you have a good story to go with the costume, but the story can be as simple as the claim that you just came from a costume party. The costume makes a great icebreaker and conversation piece. If you bring a camera, you can have people take pictures of you with all the pretty girls and you can get their phone numbers by offering to send them copies of the photos.

In fact, the camera can be a great gimmick approach all by itself. Bring along one of those disposable cameras (with a flash) and ask a girl to take a picture of you and your friends and get the girl and her friends to pose in some of the pictures with you.

Quiz games—This technique requires at least one friend to help you pull it off. There are now a variety of trivial pursuit games and other quiz games on the market. Pick one that you think would appeal to the type of girls you are trying to meet and bring a stack of the cards with you the next time you go to a bar. Pull out the cards and make a rule that when a person gets a question right, he or she gets to choose who takes a drink. Make sure that it looks like you are having a blast and invite some girls to join the game.

The Drop—This classic approach will work in an office setting, but it can be effective just about anywhere that isn't too dirty. If you are carrying a stack of papers, books or other supplies, pretend to drop them next to the girl you want to meet. Fumble around on the ground and look up at her like you need help so that when she does, you can get a chance to thank her and get her name. If she seems responsive, offer to buy her a cup of coffee, a drink or even dinner as further thanks. "Thanks, you are so nice to help. I feel like a klutz. Well, I'm (name), I work on the second floor. (pause to get her name). I don't know when I might see you again. Could I buy you a cup of coffee?"

The Direct Approach:

The direct approach works best when you have already made eye contact and she seems receptive. It's one of the riskiest ways to approach a woman but it's also the most impressive and sincere when done properly. In fact, the ultimate anti-pickup line is used in the direct approach. It's short, non-threatening and quite often gets a positive approach. What is the ultimate Anti-Line? "Hi, I'm (say your name)." Then pause for her to respond in kind. The reason this Anti-Line is so powerful is that you are offering information about yourself and not directly asking anything of her. It's the line we use when starting a casual conversation with just about anyone. It's often overlooked because it often needs a good follow-up.

"Hi, I'm (name) (pause for her name). Nice to meet you (repeat her name if she offers it)." At this point you can talk about the location, ask her about her name or even discuss the weather.

"Hello, my name is (name), I live (place). Here's my card. (pause) Good to meet you. I'd be happy to buy you a drink. What would you like? (pause)

"Hi, how are you doing? (pause) O.K. if I join you for a moment?" (pause) My name is (name). (pause)

At this point you are probably thinking, "These approaches are too basic. They are no different from starting small talk with anybody." That is exactly the point. Humor is a good thing when you meet a woman. If you can make her laugh you'll usually be ahead of the game. But, not every guy is a comedian. We need to remind ourselves that beautiful women are people just like everyone else. They appreciate a sincere and friendly person with enough confidence to just come up and say "Hi."

Step 4: The Bridge

You've already learned the principles behind The Bridge in Chapter 8, "Creating the Connection." Once you've made your initial approach, your goal is to transition into bridging the gap between the two of you by finding and focusing on things that both of you have in common. The key to The Bridge is to learn as much as you can about her while offering only carefully selected information about yourself. We tend to look for reasons to discount the other person early in the meeting process. Don't give her ammunition to discount you. Information is power. That doesn't mean you spend the night interrogating her. When you find something in common with her, you can direct the conversation to focus on that common interest.

You don't have to like the same music or the same movies. Maybe you both have a passion for your jobs or you both love to travel. Maybe you both grew up in the same city or know some of the same people. Maybe both of you love Italian food. Maybe both of you think she is gorgeous. What you have in common is not as important as finding something that you have in common. You can further cement the connection by subtly mirroring her mannerisms and vocal patterns as you learned in Chapter 8.

When you do share information about yourself, you want to be careful to be positive and brief. This is no time to bag on your ex-girlfriend or mention the problem you're having with foot fungus. Do some soul searching beforehand and think through how you want to present yourself to a new person. If you have an interesting story that presents you in a positive light, make sure you speak with emotion and use word pictures to keep the story interesting. For example: "…so I notice a guy throwing a brown burlap bag into the ocean before he drives off. Something is moving inside the bag and I thought I heard a puppy's yelp. I kicked off my shoes and jumped into the ocean to retrieve the bag. The water was pretty cold, but inside were three of the most precious little furry black and white puppies you've ever seen." A story is better than bragging about your accomplishments and connections. But you also want to keep any stories about yourself to a minimum. She would rather hear about how much you approve of her thoughts and feelings than hear about your accomplishments.

During this phase, you are carefully looking for positive cues from her. Body language is the most important consideration. Is she facing toward you? Is she twirling her hair or touching her chest? Is she making good eye contact? Did she touch you at any point in the conversation? Any of these actions are clues that you should step up the level of intimacy. When a woman gives you a positive cue, you need to take action. You can flirt with her more intensely by winking at her or holding eye contact longer than normal. You can ask her more intimate questions about what makes her feel romantic, loved or sexy. You can touch her arm or hair and linger a bit longer than you did earlier in the evening. It's called acceleration and it's a critical phase of The Bridge. Women say this is where many guys screw up because they aren't paying attention. The woman gives the guy a cue that she is ready for more intimacy and the guy fails to accelerate the flirting. You don't need to spend the whole night creating The Bridge. Once you feel like you've made a connection and accelerated the intensity, it's is time to take the next step.

Step 5: The Close

Any good salesman knows that it is the ability to "close the deal" that separates the men from the boys. Making a sale means getting the customer to sign on the bottom line. Closing the deal with a woman may mean getting a kiss, getting her to leave with you, setting up a date or getting her phone number or email address. If all fails, you should at least give her your business card so you have a chance that she will call you. The key is to at least try for something when you make a connection with a beautiful woman. A technique that will greatly improve your odds of success is to casually tell her what you want from her instead of asking her.

I saw the power of telling rather than asking during my days as a TV reporter. Reporters are often sent to a busy location to get opinions from the public about the topic of the day. Some reporters have trouble with this assignment because they ask people walking by if they want to speak on camera and most people say "no" because they are nervous about looking stupid on TV. I used a different approach. Instead of asking a person whether he wanted to speak on camera I casually told him that I needed his opinion and put my microphone in his face as I asked the question of the day. Virtually everyone answered the questions because it never occurred to them that they could easily say no.

This technique is called assuming the sale and it works as well with women as it does with interview subjects or sales prospects. Instead of asking a woman for her number, say, "I'd like to get your number so we can get together later. Why don't you write it down here?" If she offers her email address instead, don't sweat it. Many women today, especially the young ones, are used to using email as a first contact. They will often give you their phone number after you message them.

Instead of asking her to leave with you say something like this: "It's so loud in here. I know a great all-night coffee shop where we can talk. Let's get out of here."

Leaving with her doesn't have to mean that you have to get her back to your place that night. You can go to another party spot, go for a walk in the night air, or even grab a bite to eat. Once you leave together, setting up a date or getting her phone number is usually a snap because the two of you have already brought your relationship to a new environment and a new level.

When you do ask her out, offer to take her to do something you both enjoy. You should have determined what she enjoys during The Bridge portion of the conversation. Some women are hesitant to give out their number or even an email address to a man they've just met. If she declines to give you her contact information, offer yours. However, don't write your number on a napkin if you can avoid it. It's difficult to write neatly on the soft fabric and the ink will often smear. Your number does her no good if she can't read it. Always carry around extra business cards for this purpose (even if you have to get some specially made for the purpose). Write your home number on the back so she doesn't have to call you at work. Your business card is also a great way to show her you are gainfully employed. I know guys who have special business cards printed with impressive titles for themselves that they use for meeting women. A friend of mine loves to tell women he is an astronaut and he even has the NASA business cards to prove it. He did work for NASA, but he was never an astronaut. At least he could tell her the difference between G force and G spot, though it's probably best to demonstrate. When you write your home number on the back of your business card, include a friendly phrase that reminds her about you and encourages her to call:

"The great guy you met at Fridays" or "The guy who made you laugh and wants to take you on a picnic."

The Ultimate Pick-Up Strategy will put you head and shoulders above most guys trying to meet women. But even these techniques won't work with every woman. You may need an advanced approach. Some women want what they can't have. Others want to be persuaded. A few want a man to treat them like dirt. For these special cases we have provided…

Advanced Techniques for the Hard To Get

The Touch-and-Go:

Life would be a lot easier if people said what they meant and dumped all the mind games. But human nature is a funny thing. Many women like drama. That's why soap operas are so popular with those of the female persuasion. How can you bring some drama into her life? Once you make the initial contact, don't feel like you have to struggle to maintain the conversation or "close the deal" at that moment. If she seems a little cool, find an opportunity to make a polite exit. If you are at a bar or a party, you may decide to leave her for several minutes. If you met her on campus or the local health club, you might not see her for a couple of days or even a week. The important point is that when you "walk" she is going to question why you didn't keep hitting on her like all the other guys do.

Suddenly, she is a little self-conscious and you seem more interesting. When you eventually meet up with her again, greet her by name and tell her how much you enjoyed meeting her. She'll be much more intrigued than if you kept hitting on her originally. The Touch-and-Go is an expression of an attitude more than anything else. Your actions are saying that you like her but you aren't obsessed with her. She may even start to pursue you. That makes you an attractive challenge and that is a good thing to be.

The Bad Boy:

Women sometimes complain about the aggressive "jerks" they meet and date. You will notice that they keep meeting and dating these "jerks." Believe me, if there were no demand for these cocky guys, there would not be so much supply. It's much better to be the stud being complained about than the sensitive dud being complained to. Don't be afraid to express the "Bad Boy" in you. If a girl gives you a bad attitude or expresses boredom, your cocky comment or harmless insult may be just the jolt you need to get her attention. Anger and lust are two powerful emotions. Often, women get the two confused. Whether they admit it or not, many women like a challenge and love confident men who keep them on their toes. This is especially true of younger women because they haven't been burned enough to stay away from the fire.

This strategy may seem to contradict much of what you've learned from this book on how to treat a woman. But a quick comeback shows intelligence and creativity and a little aggressiveness can signal confidence. You can still be a gentleman towards her in most ways. You just want to show her that you have an edge that makes you exciting to be around. During my early single years, I helped a sexy girl get her car started and took the opportunity to ask her out on a date. I planned a romantic dinner date at an oceanfront restaurant. When I picked her up she was wearing drab business attire and ugly black-rimmed glasses. This was not the blue-collar babe I had asked out and the conversation started out awkwardly at best. Out of nervousness I made a crack about how she looked like a librarian behind those glasses. At first she was pretty pissed. But we started kidding each other about the crappy start to our date and she confessed that she was trying to act smart and sophisticated because she knew I was a college guy. I gently removed her glasses and it wasn't long before she removed those offensive clothes.

The Little Yes:

If a woman seems interested but coy, you can opt for a tried-and -true sales technique. The salesman asks a series of questions for which he knows the answer is yes. Those questions lead to the one that closes the deal. Pay attention and you'll catch salespeople using this technique often—because it works. Simply weave questions into the conversation that you know will get a positive response. After she has agreed that, "yes," it is a beautiful day and, "yes" the band is great and, "yes" she likes music, you can get her to tell you about her favorite music. You can then ask her if she might like to hear some of that music with you sometime. The same technique can work for movies, books, restaurants, recreational activities, Kama Sutra—you name it. You are selling her on something she enjoys and you just make yourself part of the deal.

The Big Question:

Believe it or not, most women hate to say no. Rejecting another person is rarely pleasant for either party. Unfortunately, a woman may also feel uncomfortable about meeting a new person for the first time so she may reject you out of a sense of initial discomfort. That is why the "Big Question" works so well. I know a guy who will meet a woman, immediately tell her she is beautiful and ask her an outrageous question like, "Will you marry me tonight?" or "How about we get out of here right now?" The woman may be momentarily startled and usually says "no," but at the same time she may be flattered and somewhat intrigued by his confidence. He then quickly follows up with a smaller request like, "Can I at least buy you a drink?" or "Will you at least tell me your name?" or "How about a dance then?" Compared to the first request, these requests seem very reasonable. Ask for the grand prize and she'll feel obligated to give you the consolation prize. But don't be too shocked if some women take you up on your first request or remind you about that request later in the night.

The Wolf Pack:

Predatory animals often hunt in packs. If you are hunting for a hard-to-get babe, you may want to try a variation of the Wolf Pack for yourself. You need at least one friend to help you with this technique. There are many variations. One guy walks up to a beautiful woman, introduces himself and persuades the woman to come with him; he has a friend who wants to meet her. The friend acts a little embarrassed about being put on the spot and thanks the woman for being such a good sport. Both guys talk to the woman and laugh at each other's jokes so there is less pressure on either guy. Many times the woman will go for the guy who first introduced himself and sometimes she may even call over a girlfriend for a little two-on-two conversation. It helps to have a good sense of humor, but the Wolf Pack works. Best of all, if the girl is unreceptive, no one feels rejected.

Anti-Lines for the wolf pack technique:

"Hi, I'm (your name.) What's your name?" (She answers), "Nice to meet you, (her name), I'm hoping you can do me a favor. My friend over there is a little shy but he's a great guy. He thinks you're cute and I know he would like to meet you. How about we go over and make his night?" Even if she doesn't want to go over to meet your friend, you've started a conversation with her yourself. If she hesitates, you can ask her what type of guy she likes. If the guy she describes sounds like you, keep the conversation moving to your advantage.

"Hey, it's my friend's birthday. Join the party. He needs a birthday hug." Some prodding may be necessary. After the hug, ask for her name and ask when her birthday is coming up. If she answers and seems to be playing along, you can offer her an early birthday hug. Sometimes this can result in a whole round of birthday hugs.

"Hi. See that guy over there. That's (your friend's name.) He's my best friend in the world and one of the nicest guys you'll ever meet. He and his girlfriend broke up a couple weeks ago and he's finally moving on. Now we're trying to get him back into the groove of meeting beautiful women. He's harmless (saying he lost his genitals in a nasty hunting accident is over the top). Help me out and come over to say hi."

The Lily Pad:

What should a guy do if he's interested in a woman who has a boyfriend? The answer lies in "The Lily Pad Theory." A good share of the female population will go to great lengths to make sure they have a boyfriend at all times. This type of woman hops from one boyfriend to another in much the same way a frog jumps from lily pad to lily pad. She isn't necessarily head over heals with the guy she is dating. She just doesn't want to be alone while she waits for Mr. Right to come within jumping distance. It may seem like a sign of insecurity that she needs a perpetual boyfriend. But these women are able to move from boyfriend to boyfriend because they have so much to offer.

If you are interested in a lady who is attached but not in love, don't let the fact that she has a boyfriend scare you off. Instead, put yourself in position to be the next lily pad by becoming her close friend. This technique takes some courage and patience. The boyfriend will probably sense your motive and it may take awhile before she makes the next jump. Date other women while you are waiting and take the time to find out the little things that make her happy. Women will tell you what makes them feel special if you ask them. So ask! You'll be ready to catch her when the other lily pad starts to sink.

Bringing Out the Big Guns:

No, I'm not suggesting you start asking out women at gunpoint. That would only work once and your second date would be in a tiny cell with a big guy named Bubba. The big guns of seduction are couples dancing, serenading and writing/reciting poetry. You may think these activities are lame, but prowess in any one of these babies gives you a distinct advantage over other guys when it comes to seducing women. Let's start with dancing. Many women believe there is a direct correlation between a man's ability to move on the dance floor and his ability to make the earth move in the bedroom. I'm not talking so much about that thing you call dancing where you stand in front of the woman and shake your arms and hips like you're having a semi-rhythmic seizure. Of course, it doesn't hurt if you are comfortable with that kind of dancing as well. Real dancing takes place when you are touching the woman, whether you are Swing Dancing, doing the Cha Cha or that dance where the woman grinds her butt into the guy's crotch (my personal favorite). Pick a style of dancing that fits your personal style and take as many classes as you need to get the moves down right. You'll find dance classes are overloaded with single women and once you can smoothly guide a woman around the dance floor, it won't take much to guide her to your place.

Serenading a woman is another "big gun" in the world of seduction. A TV news photographer that I worked with and roomed with had a big crush on a stunning brunette. He was a great guy, but it was obvious that he was too shy and conservative for this outgoing stunner. One night we all went out as friends and came up on a grand piano in the lobby of a fancy hotel. My friend sat down at the piano and told the object of his affection that he had composed a song for her. When he started to play, the melody was beautiful and so was her reaction. She melted right there in front of everyone and started to cry. They were engaged a few months later. You don't have to be a gifted composer to serenade a woman. If you learn to sing or play the guitar (or both) you'll be surprised at the seductive power of a romantic song. Poetry can have the same effect. I remember watching "The Bachelorette" on NBC when a quiet and shy Ryan put his heart on paper in a series of poems. That knockout cheerleader Trista had more than a dozen studs to choose from and I must admit I never thought the guy had a chance. Next thing you know, they are getting married on national television. Yes, it takes effort to learn how to dance, sing, play an instrument or write poetry. For most guys it's too much effort. What are you willing to do to get a woman like Trista?

Chapter 11

DINNER WAS WONDERFUL.
HOW WOULD YOU LIKE TO HAVE DESSERT ON ME?

A CRASH COURSE IN COOKING AND ENTERTAINING

Some guys never really learn how to cook. I guess they don't know enough to get started or don't care enough to invest the time to learn. A guy should know how to cook at least a few signature meals so he can be impressive in the kitchen just as he is in other areas of his life. Cooking basic meals instead of eating out or ordering in all the time can be a healthy way to save big money. Just as important, cooking at home is a suave way to get a woman closer to your bedroom. Considering the fact that there are literally thousands of great cookbooks in print, there is little reason to list a bunch of recipes here. Instead, I've provided a few cooking survival tips and some cheat-sheets for easy reference with a checklist of basic tools, terms and tips to help get you started cooking today.

Fast Food Without the Wrapper:

You don't need to run for the border or march on down to the golden arches when you want fast food. There are plenty of healthy meals you can cook at home in mere minutes.

A Good Egg—An egg is a quick, healthy and economical source of protein and hey, you have to cook her something in the morning. However, if you ask a woman how she likes her eggs and she says "fertilized," don't rely on her method of birth control. I know, that is a bad yolk. Speaking of yolks, they provide flavor and important minerals but they are also high in cholesterol. You can eat five to six egg whites a day as long as you limit your consumption of egg yolks to about one a day. A healthy way to prepare eggs as a snack is to hard-boil them.

Hard Boiled Eggs—Place the eggs in a saucepan with enough water to cover them and turn the burner on high to allow the water to boil rapidly. Turn off the burner when the water reaches a rapid boil and leave the eggs in the hot water for six minutes. Cool eggs quickly by filling the pan with cold water. This will make the eggs much easier to peel.

Soft Boiled Eggs—Leave the eggs in the hot water for only three minutes after the rapid boil and pour cold water on the eggs for only a few seconds before using a spoon to scoop the egg out of the shell. You don't want the eggs to be too runny because an undercooked egg can give you salmonella poisoning.

Scrambled Eggs—Break two eggs in a bowl for each serving. Beat the eggs slightly with a splash of milk (one Tablespoon per egg) and a dash of salt and pepper (pour the salt into your palm before adding to the eggs so you don't use too much).

Heat a dab of butter or margarine (about a tablespoon) in a shallow pan over medium heat and add the egg mixture once the butter has melted and coated the bottom of the pan. As the eggs begin to set, lift the cooked portion with a spatula so that the uncooked portion flows to the bottom of the pan. When the eggs are almost completely cooked, stir them around in the pan before serving them up.

Omelet—Prepare just like scrambled eggs but don't add milk or stir the eggs in the pan. Instead, when the eggs get a glossy look, add grated cheese and your choice of omelet goodies (sausage, mushrooms, onions, salsa, etc.) before folding the egg in half and serving hot.

Low-fat grilling—A ridged grilling pan or an electric grill such as The George Foreman Grill are perfect for cooking meat with a minimum of time and hassle. Spray a little cooking oil on the grill to minimize sticking problems and preheat the grill before adding the meat or vegetables. A good indicator that meat is done is when you push on it with a fork and the meat starts to spring back. Beef is more flavorful cooked rare or medium rare. Only cut into the meat once you are pretty sure it's done because if you cut the meat and continue cooking, the juice will drain from the cut and the meat will quickly become dry.

Grilling works great for chicken, burgers, steaks, pork chops, fish, even large slices of certain vegetables such as green peppers, zucchini and onions. Grilling adds flavor, so marinade or seasoning is optional.

Salad Secrets—You can cut up the meat you just grilled and put it on a bed of lettuce or spinach leaves for a super salad. Rinse the lettuce or spinach leaves and dry them slightly with a paper towel or salad spinner. It's important to dry the leaves somewhat so the dressing sticks better. Tear rather than cut the lettuce into bite size pieces and add slices of tomato, green peppers and onions if you have them. Add the grilled meat and a low fat dressing and you have a healthy meal with almost no hassle. Mix together a can of heated chili, a jar of salsa, a chopped tomato, ½ chopped onion, grated cheese, sour cream, corn chips and a bowl of lettuce and you have an instant Mexican salad.

Speedy Spuds—One of the fastest, easiest and healthiest ways to cook a potato is heating it in a microwave.

1. Clean the potato and stab it with a fork a couple of times so it doesn't explode during the cooking process. You know, kind of like the way your pet hamster went.

2. Cook it in the microwave on high for about three minutes. This varies with the microwave and the size of the potato. You'll know it's done when it gets soft.
3. You can give the potato that oven baked flavor by coating it with butter or olive oil and toasting the cooked potato for a couple of minutes in a toaster oven or the top shelf of a preheated regular oven.
4. Add buttery spread and pepper for seasoning. Parmesan cheese is a nice alternative.

Very Easy Vegetables—Preparation is no longer an excuse for avoiding veggies.

1. Put a big serving of frozen vegetables and a splash (¼ cup) of water in a bowl and cover (a saucer works great as a cover).
2. Place in microwave, cook on high for three minutes, stir and drain excess water.
3. Add seasoning, a buttery spread or even a splash of lemon juice or Italian dressing to enhance the flavor.

Spaghetti from "Scratch"—Spaghetti can be a whole meal if you add plenty of meat and vegetables. This meal takes about 30 minutes to make. But you can make extra and freeze the sauce for several fast feasts in the future.

1. Fry up about a pound of ground turkey (or lean hamburger meat) and drain as much fat as possible.
2. Chop into small cubes and add to the pan any or all of the following: tomato, green pepper, ½ red onion, garlic clove.
3. Add a jar or can of spaghetti sauce to the pan and mix all the contents. Reduce the heat to a simmer while you prepare the pasta.
4. Fill a large pot ½ full with water and add a quick splash of olive oil as you bring the water to a fast boil.
5. You can use any shape pasta you want. Long pasta is easier to manage if you break it in half before adding it to the water. Whole-wheat pasta is a healthy alternative to traditional pasta.

6. When the pasta becomes soft, you can sample a noodle to make sure it's ready before draining the water and adding the sauce.

Nice Rice —Brown rice is extremely nutritious, goes with many dishes and it's cheap! It takes a while to make but you can make extra and store in the refrigerator for fast meals for several days. Long-grain rice is the way to go for most dishes. It stays separate and tends to be fluffier than medium or short-grain rice. Brown rice is the most nutritious because the bran layer remains on the grain. The bran provides more protein, vitamin E, calcium, phosphorus and a bunch of other stuff your body needs. If you lose the cooking instructions on the package, these should work:

1 cup brown rice
2 ½ cups water
1 tsp. salt
4 tsp. butter

Combine the ingredients in an oiled saucepan with a tight lid and bring to a boil. Reduce heat and simmer for 45 minutes or until the liquid is absorbed and the rice is tender. Fluff with a fork and serve.

Random Cooking Hints

- Always read the recipe to the end before you start cooking because an unexpected step or missing ingredient can throw off the timing of your meal.
- Prepare all ingredients to the cooking stage so that you can start cooking them about the same time to make sure they are ready about the same time.
- Use less rather than more seasoning because you can always add more to taste.
- Taste the food before serving it.
- Olive oil is one the healthiest oils and the most flavorful, so use it whenever the flavor won't overpower the food.
- High heat and/or salt make eggs tough.
- Puncturing or salting meat that you are broiling or grilling will dry it out.
- Frying garlic until it's brown will make it bitter.

• Use microwaveable storage containers so that you can reheat the leftovers the next day. Just make sure you remember to eat the leftovers within a few days so they don't grow into something green and hairy like that new growth on your privates.

• Undercooked pork and chicken can make you sick; make sure both are cooked so there is no pink in the middle. Also, make sure to carefully wash with hot soapy water anything that touched the raw meat to get rid of any contamination.

• Don't eat eggs that have cracked shells and cook eggs well to avoid food poisoning.

Kitchen Tools

❑ Can opener

❑ Casserole dish with lid (2 or 3 quart)—Pyrex

❑ Knives (6"+ blade and 3-4" blade)

❑ Long-handled utensils such as spoons (one slotted for draining and one deep for scooping) and a spatula (plastic or wood recommended)

❑ Measuring cup (2 cups) and a set of measuring spoons

❑ Mixing bowls (large and a small)

❑ Roasting pan (13" x 9"x 2") with removable metal rack so meats don't have to sit in their own grease while cooking.

❑ Saucepan with lid (3 or 4 quart)—thick aluminum or stainless steel

❑ Skillets with lids (12" and 8")—both skillets should be thick in order to distribute the heat better. A non-stick coating will allow you to use less oil in your cooking. Use plastic or wooden utensils in the skillets so you don't scratch the coating.

❑ Strainer for draining pasta and cleaning vegetables

❑ Timer

❑ Tongs

❑ Two pot holders

❑ Pepper Grinder

Spice Is Nice and Herb Isn't Just a Guy

- BASIL has a delicate flavor that is great on tomato dishes and vegetables.
- CAYENNE is made from ground chili peppers so it makes a colorful and spicy addition to chicken and Mexican dishes.
- CHILI POWDER is a mixture of spices that can range from hot to mild and adds flavor to broiled meats, marinades and, of course, chili. When you are using chili powder, remember, if it burns going in, it's going to burn coming out.
- CHIVES are a mild onion found in the produce section that can be chopped up and used in sauces, soups and salads.
- CURRY POWDER is a mixture of spices often used in Middle Eastern and Asian food that can provide an international flair.
- DILL is an herb that adds a Scandinavian flavor to potatoes, seafood and creamed foods.
- GARLIC is a pungent ROOT that is better fresh than in the form of garlic salt or powder.
- ITALIAN SEASONING is a combination of herbs and spices perfect for single guys because it takes the guesswork out of cooking. Buy a big bottle of Italian Seasoning for economy and use on any meat or vegetable dish that needs a little extra flavor.
- OREGANO is a strong spice that makes pizza taste great and also works on many meat and vegetable dishes—as long as it's used sparingly. You also want to make sure you remember which jar has the cooking Oregano and which has the "smoking" Oregano.
- PAPRIKA is a colorful spice used as much for decoration as for its unique flavor.
- ROSEMARY smells great and adds a nice flavor to seafood, baked chicken and tomato dishes.
- SALT AND PEPPER are the staples of the spice world and often overused. Pepper is best freshly cracked and you'll taste more of the actual flavor of food if you don't smother it in salt.

• THYME is strong in flavor so a dash is all you need for stews or dishes with carrots or onions.

Coming to Terms with Cooking Terms

Bake—cook with dry heat mostly from below in an enclosed space.

Baste—moisten meat with pan juices or sauce to keep the outside from drying out.

Beat—add air to a mixture and get all the ingredients evenly mixed by using a rapid circular motion from the bottom to the top of the mixture with a fork or wire whisk.

Blend—mix two ingredients so they are evenly distributed by stirring or beating.

Rapid Boil—large bubbles burst to the surface. A rapid boil is best for cooking pasta because the water should not stop boiling.

Slow Boil—bubbles break the surface in a regular pattern. Use a slow boil on vegetables and eggs.

Simmer—bubbles break under surface. A simmer is best for sauces and other long cooking foods.

Braise—brown food in cooking oil and simmer in liquid in a pan with a tight cover.

Broil—cook under broiler or over fire. Broiling over fire is also called grilling.

Butter—rub pan or grill with butter so food will not stick and it will be easier to clean.

Chop—mince is chopping as finely as possible without grinding, dice is creating ¼" to ½" squares, cube is cutting pieces ½" to 1" square.

Crisp—raw vegetables like carrot and celery strips are crisped by soaking briefly in ice water and refrigerating. Cooked vegetables are crisped by heating under the broiler to create a crispy surface.

Dot—put small dabs of butter on food before baking or broiling.

Fry—cook in oil or butter by getting the oil hot enough so the food cooks quickly and creates a crust while absorbing as little oil as possible.

Marinate—soak food in seasoned oil or sauce to season and tenderize meat.

Pare—remove any outside covering with a blade.

Preheat—heat to cooking temperature before adding food.

Stew—cook in simmering liquid until tender.

Stock—liquid in which anything has been cooked.

Toast—brown by means of dry heat.

Whip—quickly beat air into ingredients to the point where they become fluffy.

Basics of Bartending

Let's get out of these wet clothes and into a dry martini.

– Robert Benchley

The Bar Necessities:

Liquor:

Gin—the good stuff is worth the money because it contains real juniper, which adds to the taste.

Vodka—imported vodka can be expensive but some of it's really better. Domestic vodka pretty much all tastes the same, so buy the cheapest if you are buying domestic.

Scotch and Whiskey—Most people can't tell the difference between the expensive and the not-so-expensive stuff.

Tequila—this liquor gets a bad rap because the popular brands taste terrible. Spring for a premium import or you might as well pick the cheapest stuff on the shelf.

A variety of **glassware**: short glasses, tall glasses, wine and Margarita glasses and beer mugs

Accessories and Mixers:

Cocktail shaker
Strainer
A jigger or pour tops that automatically measure the liquor
Blender

Stirring sticks
Ice bucket
Fresh limes and lemon
Rose's lime juice
Salt and pepper
Cocktail napkins
Can opener
Corkscrew
Tonic Water and Collins Mix
A variety of sodas
Orange juice
Sugar

Mix It Up

Black Russian:
1 ½ oz. vodka
¾ oz. Kahlua
Pour over ice in a short glass

Bloody Mary:
2 oz. vodka
6 oz. tomato or V-8 juice
Dash "Tabasco" sauce
1/3 tsp. fresh horseradish (optional)
½ tsp. Worcestershire sauce
¼ lime
dash of salt and pepper
celery stalk

Mix in shaker and pour into tall glass half filled with ice cubes. Squeeze lime into drink, add salt and pepper and stir briefly with celery stalk.

Cosmopolitan:
¾ oz. vodka
½ oz. Triple Sec
1 oz. cranberry juice
½ oz. lime

Mix the ingredients in a shaker and strain into a chilled highball or martini glass.

Daiquiri:
2 oz. light rum
½ oz. lime juice
½ tsp. sugar
½ cup crushed ice

Blend for 10 seconds and pour into stemmed glass

Strawberry Daiquiri:
Add 1 cup fresh or frozen strawberries

Gimlet:
1 oz. gin
1 oz. lime juice

Pour into stemmed glass

Gin and Tonic:
2 oz. gin
4 oz. tonic water
1 tbsp. lime juice

Pour over ice in a chilled tall glass. Stir and add lime.

Highball:
2 oz. whiskey
club soda or ginger ale

Pour over ice in a tall glass and stir with lemon wedge as garnish.

Long Island Iced Tea:

½ oz. Triple Sec
½ oz. rum
½ oz. gin
½ oz. vodka
½ oz. tequila

Fill shaker with cup of ice and liquor. Shake and strain into a tall glass. Fill remainder of glass with cola and garnish with lemon wedge.

Mai Tai for two:

2 oz. light rum
1 oz. Triple Sec
4 oz. passion fruit juice or mango juice or peach nectar
1 oz. dark rum

Mix the first three ingredients in a shaker and pour over ice in highball glasses. Pour 1 tbsp. dark rum into center of each glass and garnish with a lime wedge.

Margarita:

1 ½ oz. tequila
½ oz. triple sec
¾ oz. lime juice

Mix in shaker and strain into ice in short glass or blend with ½ cup crushed ice and pour into stemmed glass. Salt on rim of glass (optional)

Strawberry Margarita:

Add 1 cup fresh or frozen strawberries to margarita before blending.

Martini:

3 oz. quality gin chilled
½ tsp. dry vermouth
1 olive

Add vermouth and then gin to ice in shaker and shake vigorously for 20 seconds. Strain the martini into the glass and add olive.

Pina Colada for two:

2 oz. white rum
2 oz. cream of coconut
½ cup diced pineapple

Mix the ingredients in a blender with 2 cups of ice and pour into two tall glasses. Garnish with a slice of fresh pineapple and a cherry and serve with a colorful straw or umbrella.

Sangria for six:

1 bottle merlot or cabernet wine
¾ cup brandy or cognac
½ cup orange-flavored liqueur
½ cup orange juice
2 cups club soda
1 orange, sliced thinly
1 lemon, sliced thinly
½ cup sugar

Put fruit slices in punch bowl and stir in sugar so the sugar dissolves into the juices. Add the other ingredients and stir in about 2 cups of ice cubes.

Screwdriver:

1 1/2 oz. vodka
4 oz. orange juice

Pour into short glass filled with ice and stir

Sea Breeze:

2 oz. vodka
2 oz. cranberry juice
2 oz. grapefruit juice

Pour ingredients over ice into a highball glass and stir. Squeeze lime into drink and drop into the glass.

Tom Collins:

2 oz. gin
1 oz. lemon juice
1 tsp. powdered sugar
4 oz. soda water

Mix gin, lemon juice and sugar in a shaker and pour over ice before adding the soda water.

Whiskey Sour:

2 oz. whiskey
1 oz. lemon juice
dash of sugar

Pour into short glass and stir with lemon wedge and cherry as garnish.

Zombie for two:

3 oz. rum
½ oz. apricot brandy
1 oz. pineapple juice
juice of one lime
juice of one orange
1 tsp. powdered sugar

Mix ingredients with crushed ice in shaker and strain into tall glasses.

Three Cheers for Beer

I hate to bag on anyone's brand of beer, but most of the major domestic beers taste pretty much the same so there isn't much reason to be picky about the brand if you drink domestics. Lighter beers are usually described by their brand name or put into the category of Lager, Pils, or Pilsener. If you want a hearty beer, ask for an Ale, Porter or Stout. Whether you drink domestic, micro brew or an import, choose a beer in a dark bottle or a keg because exposure to light over time can skunk a beer. For this reason never store beer exposed to sunlight. Beer should be served 43-46 degrees for best aroma and head. We all know the importance of good head.

Pouring from a bottle—Pour out half the bottle at about a 40-degree angle into the center of a mug or glass. Do not tilt the glass when you are pouring the beer. Allow the foam to settle and pour out half of what is left. Continue to fill and enjoy.

Pouring from a keg—Tilt the glass at a slight angle so the beer enters the glass without creating too much foam. Enjoy and repeat often.

Pop the Cork

Champagne—Cheap champagne tastes cheap and it will give you a headache so avoid it at all costs. As long as you are paying for quality, you might as well chill it and open it properly. Fill a large bucket with 2/3 ice, 1/3 water and up to a ½ cup of salt. Submerge the bottle in the bucket for 20 minutes.

To open champagne: Remove wire, place cloth over cork; hold bottle at a 45-degree angle away from any people and turn the bottle, not the cork.

The Wonderful World of Wine

The most important thing you need to know about wine is to avoid buying and drinking White Zinfandel. White Zin is thought of as an unsophisticated starter wine of the underclass. Chardonnay is the most popular wine in the United States with Cabernet Sauvignon and Merlot distant challengers. Make sure you have plenty of Chardonnay and at least one bottle of Cab or Merlot on hand when entertaining.

The look, smell and feel of a wine can be almost as important to your enjoyment as the taste. So make sure to:

Smell the cork when possible to gain a hint of what to expect.

Swirl the wine in the glass slightly to stir up and unlock the aromatic components.

Smell the "nose" or "bouquet" of a wine to determine if it's fresh and clean or whether any "off" odors indicate the presence of a defect. Too much acetic acid can cause a vinegar smell, faults in the cork can cause a corky odor and too much sulfur dioxide can cause a sulfur smell.

Take in enough wine to get a good feel for its unique characteristics.

A professional server should pour just the right amount so that you can empty the tasting glass with one sip. Allow the wine to roll around in your mouth for at least a few seconds. You taste sweetness on the tip of your tongue and fruit characteristics and tannins in the middle of your tongue. The lingering aftertaste is called the finish. Pause for a moment to think about the impression the wine made before accepting or buying the bottle. Under no circumstances, say to the server, "Gee this is 12 years old, don't you have anything fresh?"

The rules of matching wine with foods are not as strict as they used to be. However, you need to know the rules before you can experiment with ways to bend them. Generally, red wines such as Pinot Noir, Merlot, Cabernet Sauvignon and Zinfandel (Zinfandel and White Zinfandel are totally different) go best with red meats such as beef and lamb, as well as pasta with red sauce. White wines such as a Dry Riesling, Sauvignon Blanc and Chardonnay go well with seafood, poultry and pasta with cream sauce, as well as most Asian foods. White Riesling and Port are among the sweet wines that go best with desserts.

Chapter 12

CAPTAIN ROMANCE STRIKES AGAIN!

CAPTAIN ROMANCE

O.K., here's the payoff that I promised in Chapter 1. We're going to talk sex—how to get sex and how to get her to beg for more sex. Congratulations for plowing through all the warm-up chapters to get here. You did read all those chapters, right? Thought so. Caught you jumping ahead after one of my promos for Chapter 12 goodies? Go back to where you left and read those other chapters immediately.

Now, let's peel back the sheets. Whoever came up with the term "just be yourself" wasn't talking about how to act on a date. This is no time to burp, fart, scratch your balls or check out other chicks. You are going to be spending both time and money on this date. Why not make sure the investment pays off? To accomplish this feat you must bring along your alter ego: "Captain Romance." He is the guy that your date wants you to be. He is prepared and confident and he pays attention to all the little details that his date cares so much about. These are the super powers that allow him to seduce her faster than a speeding locomotive and leap between her tall legs in a single bound.

Six Steps to Making the Date

1. Do your homework. Find out what she likes to do and make yourself part of the package. It's rare for a woman to turn down an invitation to a concert by her favorite band or a dinner date that includes her favorite restaurant.

2. If you call her on the phone, make sure you clearly introduce yourself and, if necessary, remind her how she knows you. If you have just met, make sure you demonstrate to her that you are safe so that she can feel comfortable going out with you. You don't want to say something like, "Don't worry I'm safe!" That will have the opposite effect. Rather, try to bring up how you just walked your dog, took your niece to swim practice or volunteered at the senior center. Some guys can take this too far. Bragging about your quilting prowess may not have the desired effect.

3. Take a friendly and casual approach. Even if you are talking on the phone, remember to smile. Your smile comes across in your voice and makes you less threatening. You also want to focus on keeping your voice relaxed and in the low range. When you are nervous, your muscles tense up and that includes the muscles in the throat. This can make your voice sound high-pitched and even screechy. Take a few deep breaths and give yourself a moment to compose yourself before making the call. Think about how a guy would talk if he weren't nervous at all and then use that approach. Finally, if she seems hard-to-get, you can always play down the date aspect by telling her you planned to go out anyway and thought she might have fun coming along. Even if she isn't feeling an initial attraction toward you, it's possible to change the way she feels during the date.

4. Offer two pleasant options so "no" is not an obvious option. For example: "I was thinking it might be fun to check out that new Italian restaurant but the weather is so nice maybe a picnic at the park

would be good. What do you think would be more fun?" If she likes both options, you make the choice. Women hate wimpy guys who can't make a decision. Next, offer a broad time period. "Would this weekend be good for you?" Finally, narrow the time down further. "How does Friday night sound?"

5. Remove her concerns. Once you firm up an activity and a time, it's a good idea to give her some specifics so that she will know how to prepare for the date. Tell her what time you'll pick her up and what time she can expect to be home. You may want to give her a broad indication of what she should wear by letting her know how you plan to dress considering the formality of the activity and possible temperature and weather considerations.

6. Show your appreciation. End the conversation by letting her know that you are looking forward to the date and assure her that she's going to have a great time.

Once you secure the date it's important to plan and prepare the details. So few guys pay attention to the details that it really makes you stand out from the crowd when you do.

Pre-date Checklist:

- ❑ Plan at least two activities for the date and have a backup plan to account for weather problems.
- ❑ Make sure your car and your home are clean and stocked with condoms.
- ❑ Shower, shave, brush your teeth and style your hair.
- ❑ Check mirror for nose, eyebrow, ear and neck hair and trim if needed.
- ❑ Make sure clothes are clean, pressed and appropriate for the occasion.
- ❑ Carry a watch, wallet and plenty of money.
- ❑ Psyche yourself up by telling yourself how great the date is going to go and picture the successful date in great detail.
- ❑ Plan at least three seduction questions and at least one follow-up question for each one:

What would you say was your happiest experience? What made it so happy for you?

Can you remember a moment when you felt really loved? What was the most special thing about that moment?

What was the most exciting thing you've ever done? How did that make you feel?

If money were no object, what would be your most romantic evening?

Is romance important to you? Why?

Have you ever had a truly amazing sexual experience? Can you tell me some of the highlights? How did that experience make you feel? (These questions may be a little racy for a first date. But that depends on the girl.)

Captain Romance leaves home early to make sure that he shows up on time for the date and never complains when he is kept waiting because he realizes that women believe getting dressed and putting on makeup while the man waits is a form of dating foreplay. He also brings flowers or another gift to the first date and any fancy date thereafter.

Popular Gifts:

Chocolate—contains chemicals that act as a subtle pleasure drug.

CD of her favorite music or of the band you are about to see in concert—great gift for a music lover.

Stuffed animal or cute toy—she'll cuddle it and hopefully get in the mood to cuddle you.

Book—the educated girl will approve that you appreciate her mind as well as her body.

Card—I don't know why, but women love those stupid greeting cards.

Poem—it should not include the word "Nantucket."

Massage oil (usually not for the first date—but again, it depends on the girl).

O.K., back to Captain Romance. The big "R" offers to help his date put on her coat and he carefully checks to make sure that it's on straight.

He is decisive about where they go and what they do but he's also flexible if she expresses another preference.

He takes his date to places where he is known so that he looks popular. He appears gracious by introducing her to people he knows.

The Art of Introductions

Always name the most respected party first. "Mr. President, I'd like you to meet Monica."

Use the following hierarchy:

1. Rank, regardless of sex
2. Women
3. Eldest

Men shake hands with one another, but a man only shakes hands with a woman if she offers first. It's helpful to add a conversation starter when you introduce two people. "Mr. President, this is Monica. She is a big fan of your internship program."

Back now to the escapades of Captain Romance. He always opens doors for his date, stands when she leaves or rejoins the table and generally treats her like a princess.

Captain Romance never complains how much something costs and never makes a big deal out of the fact that he is picking up the tab. There are ways to save money on a date but this is no time to look cheap.

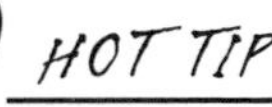

How to figure a 20% tip in two seconds:

1. Divide the pre-tax total by 10. 10% of a $55.50 tab is roughly $5.50

2. Double the amount for a 20% tip. $5.50 x 2 = $11 Subtract a dollar or two if there were serious flaws in the service.

Captain Romance looks for opportunities to make The Grand Gesture. Buying wine by the bottle instead of the glass, buying her a flower if they pass a flower stand or buying her a memento of their date even if it's overpriced.

He offers his coat when his date shows the slightest indication of being chilly and protects her fearlessly from any threat of harm or inconvenience.

He is relaxed and confident when she looks in a clothing or jewelry store window and points to the nicest item to say how great it would look on her.

He is careful to never discuss date killers such as religion, political beliefs or his old girlfriends.

He downplays the effort that went into planning the date because he knows the whole process should look easy and effortless.

He touches her casually and non-sexually at least three times during the date to create a physical connection and make her accustomed to his touch. He may lightly touch her arm while they are walking, touch her hand as he hands her a drink or makes a point and he may softly brush her hair out of her face. If she touches him or uses her body language and words to express her interest, he takes this as a clue to increase the frequency and sensuality of his touching and other displays of intimacy such as compliments and kissing. If she reaches under the table and grabs him between the legs, he shows her why they call him the man of steel. Let's hear it for Captain Romance!

He works to make her feel special by looking into her eyes a fraction of a second longer than normal before glancing at another part of her face. However, he does not stare. That creeps people out.

He remembers to make a point of casually giving her three to four compliments that are non-sexual and sincere such as, "You look beautiful tonight." And, "I'm having a great time. I hope you are too."

He asks her questions, pauses before responding and repeats back a summary of her answers in his own words to make sure she knows that he is listening to her. The response should start something like, "So, are you saying _________?"

He makes sure that the majority of the conversation is focused on her and things the two of them have in common.

He weaves his previously planned romance questions into the conversation to help her feel sensual and sexy. He starts with nonsexual questions such as: "What makes you happy?" When the time is right he generates some heat with questions such as: "How do you know when you are really turned on?"

He goes in for a kiss when he feels that the date is going especially well and he doesn't ask for permission. Captain Romance knows women love to be kissed and they respect men who go after what they want.

At the end of the date he thanks her for her company, tells her how much he enjoyed the date and promises to call for another date if that is his intention.

I bet you are thinking, "Man, I'll be unstoppable with these dating techniques, but how am I going to afford such terrific dates?" Don't worry, if you are light on dough, we'll show you how to make up for it in creativity.

Three Great $30 Dates

The Deli Picnic—Go to a good local deli before the date and buy a box of upscale crackers along with small quantities of cheeses, deli meats, and fancy salads. Of course, this won't work if your date is a Vegan. And why are you dating a Vegan anyway? She better be hot! Tell the person behind the counter that you want just enough so that you and your date can taste a variety of items. The clerk will be happy to give you suggestions on what to buy. Spend $20 on the food and another $10 on a decent bottle of wine. If neither you nor your date has a picnic basket, you'll have to improvise with a backpack or a small cooler. Bring the napkins, utensils, corkscrew and wine glasses and a blanket from home.

Take your date to the nicest natural setting you can find. It's best to pick a spot beforehand so you look prepared. Choose a site that is relatively secluded and requires a short walk to get there. However, if the weather turns bad you can lay the blanket out in your living room and have your picnic there. During the picnic, play proud host by preparing the meal for her and create intimacy by feeding her from time to time. If the conversation starts to lag, you can always talk about the wine, the different types of food and your experience in buying them for her.

The Playground—A park playground makes a great location for a fun date. Spend half of your money on flowers but keep with the theme of your date by purchasing daisies or wildflowers. You can buy her an ice cream cone or bring a container of some lemonade or punch spiked with vodka to help you stay cool and refreshed on this fun-filled date. If there is a pond nearby, you can show off your nurturing side by bringing some stale bread for feeding the ducks. The highlight of this date is the playground equipment. Climbing on the equipment and sliding down the slide together will help bring out her playfulness and may help spark happy childhood memories for her. Pushing her on the swing is an especially good way to create a bond between the two of you. What other dating activity gives you permission to push on her ass over and over again? Depending on her personality, you may want to push her just hard enough to get her heart racing. The excitement you create is a subtle form of foreplay that could help get her in the mood for some swinging times later in your bedroom. However, never push her so hard that she becomes frightened. You want her to be aroused by you, but still trust you. A bonus of this date is that you'll be so busy playing that you won't have to struggle to maintain a big conversation. A great topic when you need one is her happiest childhood memories. A bonus of this date is that you may get an opportunity to show off how well you interact with the children who are playing at the park. Women melt over guys who get along well with children.

The Drive—This date works especially well if you have a relatively nice car or a motorcycle. Find a reasonably priced restaurant that is out of the way so that you need to take a winding road through the country or mountains to get there. When you are driving over the winding road, go a little faster than normal to show her your prowess behind the wheel. You don't need to take unnecessary risks but you should strive to get her heart beating and adrenalin flowing. Again, these conditions mimic the feeling of sexual arousal, which will help her associate those feelings with you.

When you get to the restaurant and start looking at the menu, ask her what she is going to order. When she answers, tell her how much you like that meal and mention that you really are not that hungry.

Suggest that it might be more romantic if the two of you shared the meal. Order water for yourself "because you don't want to drink and drive." The shared meal will help you save money and gives you an opportunity to sit closer to her and feed her from time to time. A couple of good topics of conversation include the most exciting experience each of you ever had in a car and the most interesting place either of you ever visited in a car (that amazing romp you had with the McGee twins will have to stay in the old memory bank). If the mood is right, you can stop at a special secluded spot that you picked out earlier so the two of you can open a bottle of wine and sit and "talk" on the blanket that you just happened to bring along.

A Dozen More Great Dates

A nature walk—make sure she is the nature type and not plagued by outdoors allergies.

Museum—go yourself first to get a feel for the place and to learn something about the exhibits and artists.

Concert or music festival—make sure she likes the music that will be playing.

Beach—the water can be very seductive.

Amusement park—the rides will get her blood flowing in a way that mimics the early stages of sexual arousal (are you noticing a recurring theme?). Get her blood flowing!

Drive-in movie—works best if your vehicle has a bench seat and the movie is less riveting than your kissing.

Hot tub—nothing is hotter on a date than a few drinks with a beautiful woman in a hot tub.

Theater—classy date that makes you look cultured.

Zoo or aquarium—the animals and sea creatures will remind her that we are all animals with primitive urges. If the chimpanzees can monkey around with abandon, why not you?

Bike ride—gets her blood flowing and puts pressure on that special area you want stimulated.

Wine festival - if possible, take a bus to these events so that you can enjoy all the wine you want without fear of a DUI.

Dinner at your place (a little presumptuous for a first date)—you control the environment with close proximity to your bedroom.

As long as we are covering the "do" dates, we might as well touch on the "don'ts."

Don't Do Dates

A sporting event or a sports bar unless she is a fan—both are big turn-offs for many women.

Hollywood movie—you will have little time for interaction.

Any place where there will be lots of guys who may hit on her—who needs the competition?

An overnight trip (unless the two of you are already intimate)—too presumptuous.

The Better Bachelor Pad

You've wined her, you've dined her or maybe you just picked her up in a bar. Whatever the case, you've gone to a lot of trouble to get her back to your place. If it looks like a scene from Animal House, you may have trouble getting to first base. If you haven't seen Animal House, rent it. It's a true classic. Now back to your pad. Your home must be relatively clean and odor free, especially your bathroom and your sheets. Reduce the clutter in your home and make sure you display pictures of your family and friends. These pictures show you aren't a loner and they help her to trust you.

Healthy houseplants are a plus because they show that you are responsible and have the ability to nurture. Hey, I won't tell if you buy the plant the day before your date. What is the secret to keeping houseplants healthy anyway? The biggest error guys make involves watering. They either over-water or forget to water for weeks at a time. Set a time once a week to put your finger into the soil. If the soil is damp, don't water. If the soil is mostly dry, water thoroughly and make sure you pour out the water that collects in the saucer below the pot. If the soil is very dry, soak the whole pot for 30 minutes. Remove any dead leaves from the plant and add a little houseplant fertilizer once a month. Keep the instructions on the plastic stake that comes with the plant for more specific instructions regarding the plant.

Now, back to your bachelor pad. Avoid overusing the color black on your furnishings and decorations. The color black is a bachelor pad cliché that tells women you lack imagination. Hide those pinup posters, racy calendars and raunchy men's magazines. And make sure you hide Betty the blow-up doll. Harsh lighting with exposed bulbs or florescent bulbs will also turn her off. Make sure your bachelor pad has soft lighting and have some candles ready to help set the mood. The bar and the refrigerator should be well stocked so you can offer her a drink and possibly a snack.

HOT TIP

Make sure the answering machine volume is turned all the way down so she won't hear another woman leaving a message for you.

You should have a decent stereo and it helps if you are playing romantic music that she enjoys. If the mood is right, you can give her a tour of your place and save the bedroom for last. Speaking of the bedroom, the bed should be large with at least two pillows. Pay extra for quality linens. No synthetic fabrics! Make your bed as inviting to her as possible.

Tips for Loose Lips

Women love to kiss and they love to tell their friends they got kissed. Some guys make the mistake of asking permission before going in for the kiss or warning the woman that a kiss is coming. It's better to use your Captain Romance techniques to prime the pump and go in for the kiss when you sense the time is right. There are usually three hurdles you must cross before a woman will want to kiss you: trust, arousal and some sense of privacy. Your Captain Romance techniques will go a long way toward helping her trust you as long as they seem sincere to her. That means you should avoid probing her tonsils for now.

Sometime during the date you also want to get her aroused. There are ways to accomplish this even before the physical contact with her begins and I provide several examples in the list of great dates. Wearing a red shirt or having her eat spicy food can get her heart pumping a little faster. When possible, try something more dramatic. Take her on an amusement park ride, take her to a scary movie, sneak her into someplace that is supposed to be closed, push her on a swing, take her to the top of a tall building or mountain, take her horseback riding or bike riding. If you can get her to ride a mechanical bull, you should have no problem getting her to ride you. Physical arousal is very similar to sexual arousal so it's not a big step for her to make.

The touching techniques and romantic questions you learned early in this chapter are some of the best ways to get her in the mood. You can prime the pump with a touch on her hand or arm and a question such as, "Do you remember your first great kiss?" That question can be followed later by, "What made it so special?" The final key to your success with her is to get her somewhere private where she will feel comfortable getting more intimate. Take her someplace on a walk or a drive where the two of you can be alone. Even a crowded bar or party might work if she feels that no one is paying attention. Her place or your place is the ultimate as long as family members or roommates won't be barging in.

Once you have crossed the three hurdles of trust, arousal and privacy, give her a nonsexual compliment such as, "You look beautiful tonight" or "I'm having fun. Thanks for taking this walk with me." If she likes you, she'll generally give you clues that her lips are longing for some contact. She'll smile more and she'll look into your eyes. She'll turn her face and body toward you more and she may tilt her head when she listens to you. She might play with her hair or lightly touch her chest. Any of these clues can be a green light that it's time for some lip lock.

When she responds in a positive manner, look into her eyes and slowly move closer or gently pull her toward you. People's kissing styles and preferences vary greatly. If she dresses and acts aggressively you may be able to take that as a clue that she'll want a more aggressive kiss right up front. Usually, however, it's best to begin the kiss gently. As you move in, slowly tilt your head to one side so she has time to tilt her head to the other side. Kiss her mouth softly with your lips parted only slightly.

After the initial contact, your mouth can open a bit more with the tip of your tongue at the entrance to your mouth. Your tongue is probably larger than hers so you want to point the tip somewhat and be cautious about putting too much of your tongue into her mouth. Make small circular, figure eight and in-and-out motions with your tongue and glide your tongue along her tongue. Don't feel like you have to tangle tongues the whole time. Kiss her upper and lower lip with your lips from time to time. The important thing is to mirror her kissing style as much as possible. Alternate from kissing her mouth to her ears, neck and hands. If her shoulders are exposed you'll want to spend some time there as well. As you move back to her mouth you can enjoy deeper tongue-to-tongue kisses and more prolonged kisses on the lips. Some light caressing is fine at this point. But don't hurry to remove her clothes or reach for the goodies just yet.

A woman's body responds differently to stimulation than yours. While your response to passion can be compared to a microwave oven with a simple on/off switch, she is more like a slow-cook crock-pot with a complicated array of knobs and buttons. If you take the time to kiss her and softly caress her, she'll eventually become aroused and desire more. Hold her close and stay away from the breasts and genitals at first. Remember that a woman's skin is more sensitive than yours. Don't rub the same area over and over. Instead, let your hands and mouth glide softly over different parts of her body. Make a mental note of touches that seem to increase her arousal and then return to those areas more often. You may find she starts touching herself or moving your hand to areas that need attention. You can also get clues by where and how she is touching you. Try touching her in the same areas and in the same way that she is touching you and move your body with hers like a horizontal dance. This is a variation of the "mirror" technique from Chapter 8. It will make her feel like the two of you are completely in sync with each other.

Give her sincere compliments about her beauty and how good she makes you feel. At this point you can even compliment specific body parts as long as you take a sensual rather than a crude approach. Telling a woman she has nice legs or nice breasts will get you much farther than saying she has great hooters and you'd like to jump on the junk in her trunk.

Playing with the Goodies

Believe me, the breast is yet to come. When you feel that she is responding to your kissing and touching, you may want to gently move your hand to one of her milky white orbs of love (the topic of breasts gets me a little carried away). Start by gliding your hand along the side of a breast and then move your hand away to touch other parts of her body. This should tease her into wanting more. Eventually, you can move your hand back and spend more time on both breasts. Some women have very sensitive breasts, especially in the nipple area, so you'll want to be extra gentle and vary your rubbing and soft squeezing. This touching can progress naturally to the skin under her clothes. Don't jerk or tug at her clothes. Focus on making smooth movements as you glide your hand under her top or up her dress.

Spend some time on her thighs before moving to your final destination. If she is moaning or her body is writhing, it may be time to lightly touch the skin of her breasts and between her legs. Don't linger too long at first. Lightly glide your hand over the area and move back to another part of her body. It's a good idea to maintain occasional eye contact during this process and continue kissing her mouth, face, neck and shoulders so she knows that you are focused on her and not just her breasts and that special area between her legs.

HOT TIP

Being able to gently unhook her bra with one hand is a must for a Modern Alpha Male. Some bras have a plastic clasp in the front between the two cups. For this type of bra, slip your forefinger between her breasts and under the clasp. Use your thumb and middle finger to push the sides of the clasp down around your forefinger. This will cause the clasp to snap open. Use your fingers to guide the unclasped bra apart gently so it doesn't abruptly snap apart. Most bras hook in the back. Find where the ends hook together and isolate the bra's tension between your forefinger on one side and your thumb and other fingers on the other side. Slide your thumb across the clasp, releasing the hooks. Let the unhooked straps separate gently.

Don't be in a rush to take off her panties. Rather, enjoy the texture of the panties against her skin and allow your fingers to slide over the panties with smooth gentle movements. You'll want to vary your touch. A circular motion can be followed by gentle back and forth rubbing and even "S" patterns. This isn't paint by numbers. Do what feels right. Just don't continuously rub the same area in the same way or it will quickly become irritating to her. When the panties come off, this variety of touching becomes especially important.

It's critical when using your tongue around her nether regions. Some guys spell out the alphabet with their tongue down there to keep the stimulation varied. You'd be surprised how many women love their ABC's. Remember, it's very easy to over stimulate a woman's clitoris. You should only touch it lightly and infrequently at first. Don't focus on it too much until she tells you or shows you that she wants more. Making a woman beg for more is not a bad thing. If she appears ready to orgasm you can spend a little more time softly rubbing and or licking the clitoris but lighten up on that area once she hits the big "O."

Another hot button that needs careful attention is the so called "G spot." There is some controversy about whether this area is truly the key to female orgasms, but it's certainly a sensitive spot that appreciates attention. The "G spot" is an area of spongy tissue located on the front-inside wall of her vagina. This tissue protects her urethra, which is a very sensitive part of her body. You reach the area by letting your curved middle finger glide up the front-inside wall of her vagina until the angle and texture starts to change to a more spongy consistency. If you are not sure, ask her what area seems to feel best. A few gentle circles and "S" patterns on the "G spot" alternated with some rubbing of the vaginal lips and clitoris and you should have her moaning for more.

Everybody Out of the Pool

Professor: Every fifteen minutes in the U.S. some student is contracting VD.

Coed: I think I know him.

—Melvin Helitzer

The foreplay techniques you've learned will certainly make it difficult for a woman to say no to having sex with you. This is a responsibility as well as an opportunity. Wearing a condom is a must, and even a condom won't protect you from herpes or genital warts. Plus, condoms can leak, break and fall off. You probably know all this stuff but it's worth repeating. Finally, there is the emotional baggage that comes with becoming sexually intimate with another person. I don't want to be a downer, but you really need to weigh these consequences before having sex with a woman. You also need to respect her wishes if she starts having second thoughts. At this stage of the game "no" is a really big deal. No means no and stop means stop, even if her actions seem to say "yes" and "go." In fact, if you put on the brakes when she gives you the red light, you may find her more willing to give you the green light as she becomes more comfortable with you. Never plead or try to beg your way into bed. It makes you submissive and unattractive and it rarely works. Even if it does, the sex will be lousy and you'll both probably regret the experience afterward.

The Final Frontier

I said to my wife "All things considered I'd like to die in bed," and she said, "What, again?"

—Rodney Dangerfield

Let's assume you've taken the right precautions, she's the one for you and you've followed the steps above until she is begging for your little soldier. Forget every porno movie you've seen and the dirty stories you've read. This is no time to "lunge at her with your mighty manhood" or "thrust at her like a human battering ram." Those male fantasies frighten and disgust most women in real life. Instead, think passionate instead of aggressive and take the time to tease her into wanting more. First, grab private one-eye in your hand and gently rub his helmet along the lips of her vagina and around her clitoris for at least 20 seconds. If the area seems moist enough, slowly slide the head in a few times. Eventually, you'll want to enter her about an inch for several more strokes.

Slowly increase the depth while resisting the urge to go in all the way. Occasionally mix up your repertoire by going back to entering just as deep as the head of your penis. This should have her begging for more and trying to pull you in all the way. Give her a little more but don't submit right away. You are in control. Continue your teasing until she seems to be on the verge of orgasm. Even then, be careful never to ram your pelvic bone into her clitoris because this can over-stimulate this very sensitive area and it will certainly ruin her mood.

While the missionary position is a good place to start, switch to other positions every time you feel you are getting close to your own orgasm. Make the transition to other positions with finesse like the smooth operator that you are and be willing to laugh at yourself if there is a temporary awkward moment like the two of you falling off the bed. Switching positions will help you last longer and make it more interesting for both of you. The exception is if she is on the edge of orgasm and demanding more of you. She may lose her moment if you stop right when she is reaching her peak.

Focus on maintaining a smooth rhythm and slowly allow yourself to increase the speed and depth of your thrusts as her expressions of passion increase. Tell her and show her that you are willing to do what she likes. That may include stimulating her with your fingers or letting her get on top. Not all women orgasm during sex, but you'll greatly increase your odds by using these techniques. Even if you've got her warmed up with 20 minutes of foreplay, she'll generally need at least ten minutes of stimulation to reach the "big O" during intercourse. On the other hand, more than 30 minutes of nonstop intercourse can be too much for some women.

Remember, ladies come first. Once she has reached orgasm or she seems completely satiated you can finally lose control and let your soldier fire his first shot. After your orgasm, resist the temptation to pass out or to ask her how good you were. Instead, give her some genuine compliments and gentle attention and kisses to make sure she feels appreciated while you give yourself some time to rally for round two. If you are an older guy, this is a good time to reminisce to yourself about the days when you could rally for round two.

Work it Out or Get Out

Whenever you are dating women there are going to be problems. It's just a fact of life. Some problems can be fixed and others cannot. You need to be able to spot the difference. Here are suggestions on how to handle some of the common problems you'll face with women.

Crying—Women cry for a variety of reasons. If a woman you are dating cries a lot for apparently irrational reasons, she is probably unstable and you'll do best to cut bait. If a woman has a legitimate reason for crying, it's usually best to hold her and wipe or kiss away her tears. She mostly wants you to listen to her. Soothe her and tell her you hear and understand her so that she knows you are listening to her. Don't offer her advice. Women want you to listen to their problems, not try to solve them.

Moodiness—Fluctuations in hormones can make some women act moody. Other women have learned to use their moods to get what they want. You can have empathy for the fact that she has mood swings without taking them personally or rewarding her for being in a bad mood. Don't jump to accommodate her every demand or give her anything she wants just because she is in a mood. If she expresses a problem, you can listen and acknowledge the problem. But don't let it pull you into a fight or pull down your positive attitude. A good approach is to ignore her when she is expressing bad behavior and reward her with attention when she is behaving better. Give her space to deal with her own problems and moods.

Jealousy—First, you need to get to the root of her jealousy. If you have wandering eyes and flirt with other women in her presence, she has reason to be jealous. A woman deserves your attention when you are with her. If her jealousy seems irrational or it was caused by an experience of her past, it's best to avoid her when she becomes jealous to discourage her negative behavior.

Criticism—If a woman criticizes you on rare occasions, you can acknowledge the criticism by repeating back what she said in your own words. If you feel the criticism is justified, you can offer to change, but usually it's enough for her to know you heard her by saying something like, "So what you're saying is ___________. That's good to know. I didn't know you felt that way." Some people criticize others habitually. If you get hooked up with a professional critic, it's best to stand up for yourself and say something like, " I don't want to hear it" or "I don't like to be talked to that way. O.K.?" Show her the door if the criticism persists.

How to Cut Bait

There are a lot of bad ways to break up with a woman and even the best ways will only minimize the pain.

- Break up with her in person.
- Put the blame on yourself. Say it's your problem or say you aren't ready for such a serious relationship.
- Compliment her to boost her now fragile ego.
- Let her know that your decision is final and tell her you feel it's is better to break up now rather than postpone the inevitable.
- Comfort her only briefly before suggesting she talk with a friend.

When You Find a Keeper

To have twenty lovers in one year is easy. To have one lover for twenty years is difficult.

—Zsa Zsa Gabor

Our thirteenth President, Calvin Coolidge, and his wife were touring a government farm. When Mrs. Coolidge passed the chicken pens she asked about the sexual habits of the rooster. Her guide proudly proclaimed that the rooster copulated dozens of times a day. "Please tell that to the president," she said. When the president passed the pens he was told about the rooster and Mrs. Coolidge's comment. He asked, "Same hen every time?" "Oh no, Mr. President, a different one each time." The president nodded and said, "Tell that to Mrs. Coolidge."

This little story illustrates what animal breeders and scientists have often observed. In many species of animal, the male eventually loses his arousal for one female and quickly regains his arousal when another female is brought into the picture. Breeders of prize bulls will introduce a variety of cows to a bull to increase his seminal output. A male rat will mate with a female rat half a dozen times before exhausting his sexual stamina. Introduce another female and that rat is suddenly ready to romp again. If you've ever seen chimpanzees monkeying with each other at the zoo, you know they are the true swingers of the animal kingdom. Maybe that is why the word monogamy starts to sound like monotony to many guys. Seen on the wall of a woman's restroom: "Show me a beautiful woman and I'll show you a guy who is sick of fucking her." Don't let the Coolidge Effect ruin a great relationship for you. Eventually, you will meet Miss Right and the two of you will spend more and more time together. At first everything seems perfect, with a great emotional connection and fantastic sex. It may come in several months or even several years, but you should be prepared for the time when some of the original thrill starts to fade. This is when some guys cut bait and run. Don't lose a great girl because of this natural genetic urge to merge with a variety of women. A good monogamous relationship can make you happier than you can imagine, but it takes work and the work involves finding new ways to keep the spark alive.

Early in a relationship you hear a lot about being "in love," but at some point you need to focus on "making love" even when you are outside of the bedroom. I'm not talking about bending her over the living room couch or taking her into the kitchen for a taste of her cherry pie, although those activities certainly won't hurt. One of the best ways to keep your own fire burning is to focus on what you can do to keep the relationship interesting and romantic for her. When you take charge of the romance in your relationship, it puts you in the dominant Alpha Male role. You may not always feel like being romantic, but when you push yourself to make the effort, it won't take long before the feelings follow. Then, when she starts showing you her appreciation, you'll really start to feel it!

Top Ten Ways to Fire Up a Relationship

1. Ask her to tell you specifically what makes her feel loved and do it.
2. Truly listen to her without trying to solve her problems.
3. Surprise her with thoughtful presents and romantic trips.
4. Read sexy stories to her and watch sexy (not raunchy, unless she's into that) videos with her.
5. When she does something great, lavish her with praise and make sure you bite your tongue when she does something that bugs you.
6. Write her a brief love note or a poem.
7. Give her a candlelight bubble bath.
8. Call her for no reason other than to tell her that you are thinking of her.
9. When you are out with her, flirt with her and focus on her like she is the only person that matters.
10. *Buy the Book 1001 Ways To Be Romantic* for 991 more ideas.

Once you can maintain the excitement and romance in a relationship with the woman of your dreams, you will have successfully survived being a single guy. You'll no doubt find that you've learned secrets and developed qualities that enrich your life far beyond the ability to meet and seduce women. You have gained more wealth, status, and a new level of physical excellence in your life. You have learned to develop your mind and gained the ability to get what you want. You understand the power of commitment and the importance of seeking compatibility with others. And hopefully, you've had a hell of a lot of fun along the way. You can also find even more hot tips at www.singleguysurvival.com. Now go tell your single friends about The Single Guy's Survival Guide. Let's face it, single guys need help, and this book is it.

BIBLIOGRAPHY

Body for Life by Bill Phillips. HarperCollins Publishers: 1999. An effective program to transform your body in 12 weeks.

The Evolution of Desire by David M. Buss. Basic Books: Revised edition 2003. A comprehensive explanation of the science behind the strategies of human mating.

How to Pick Up Women by Eric Weber with Molly Cochran. Symphony Press: 1979. The sequel to How to Pick Up Girls that takes you to the expert level of meeting women.

How to Satisfy a Woman Every Time...and have her beg for more! by Naura Hayden. Bibli O'Phile Publishing: 1982. Step-by-step technique for bringing a woman to orgasm.

How to Succeed with Women by Ron Louis and David Copeland. Prentice Hall: 1998. Your road map to a woman's heart.

Love Signals by Dr. David B. Givens. Pinnacle Books: 1985. How to present and read body language when meeting the opposite sex.

The Modern Man's Guide to Life by Denis Boyles, Alan Rose, Alan Wellikoff and a bunch of other guys. Harper and Row: 1987. Advice and information for men.

Queer Eye for the Straight Guy by Ted Allen, Kyan Douglas, Thom Filicia, Carson Kressley, and Jai Rodriguez. Clarkson Potter/Publishers: 2004. The Fab 5's guide to looking better, cooking better, dressing better, behaving better and living better.

10 Secrets for Success with Beautiful Women by Ursula Lindstrom. Samarkand Publishing: 1999. A complete how-to guide for pursuing the women of your dreams.

1001 Ways to be Romantic by Gregory Godek. Casablanca Press Division of Sourcebooks: 1999. Ideas and resources for transforming your relationship into a vibrant, exciting love affair.

Index

Symbols

A

B

C

J

K

L

M

N

O

P

The Single Guy's Survival Guide
Order Form

Fax orders: 805-773-4990
Postal Orders: Jackson Douglas Press
P.O. Box 3196
Shell Beach, CA 93448
Telephone orders: 1-800-472-5904
On-line orders: www.singleguysurvival.com

Name ______________________________
Company ______________________________
Street address ______________________________
City ______________________________
State ______________ Zip ______________
Telephone ______________________________
E-mail address ______________________________

Total books ordered: ______ $19.95 each
Sales tax:
7.75% for books shipped
to California addresses ______ ($1.55/book)
Shipping & Handling*
(per location):
$4.00 for the first book ______
$1.00 each additional book ______
Total enclosed $ ______

Payment:

Check or money order (Make payable to: Jackson Douglas Press)
Credit Card: ❑ VISA ❑ MasterCard
Card number: ______________________________
Exp. Date: __________ Signature ______________________
Name on card ______________________________
*shipping charges to non-U.S. addresses will be higher.

The Single Guy's Survival Guide
Order Form

Fax orders: 805-773-4990
Postal Orders: Jackson Douglas Press
P.O. Box 3196
Shell Beach, CA 93448
Telephone orders: 1-800-472-5904
On-line orders: www.singleguysurvival.com

Name____
Company____________________________________
Street address ________________________________
City ____
State __________________ Zip __________________
Telephone ___________________________________
E-mail address ________________________________

Total books ordered:	______	$19.95 each
Sales tax:		
7.75% for books shipped		
to California addresses	______	($1.55/book)
Shipping & Handling*		
(per location):		
$4.00 for the first book	______	
$1.00 each additional book	______	
Total enclosed	$ ______	

Payment:

Check or money order (Make payable to: Jackson Douglas Press)
Credit Card: ❑ VISA ❑ MasterCard
Card number: ________________________________
Exp. Date:__________ Signature ____________________
Name on card _________________________________
*shipping charges to non-U.S. addresses will be higher.